Hotel Renaissance
19 Rue Du Parnasse
1050 Brussels

BOLT FROM THE B

BOLT FROM THE BLUE

Navigating the New World of Corporate Crises

Mike Pullen and John Brodie Donald

*For Yoko,
who fell
as cherry blossoms must*

(John Brodie Donald)

*To Rebecca and Michelle
– a stellar team with unlimited potential*

(Mike Pullen)

First published 2014 by
Elliott and Thompson Limited
27 John Street, London WC1N 2BX
www.eandtbooks.com

ISBN: 978-1-90965-330-6

Copyright © Mike Pullen and John Brodie Donald 2014

The views expressed in this book are the views of the authors and do not necessarily reflect the views of DLA Piper.

All rights reserved. No part of this publication may be reproduced, stored in or introduced into a retrieval system, or transmitted, in any form, or by any means (electronic, mechanical, photocopying, recording or otherwise) without the prior written permission of the publisher. Any person who does any unauthorized act in relation to this publication may be liable to criminal prosecution and civil claims for damages.

Picture credits:
Page 46: diagram from the report of the Presidential Commission on the Space Shuttle Challenger Accident (PCSSCA), volume v, p. 896 (1986)
Page 47: diagram redrawn from Edward Tufte, *Visual Explanations*, Graphics Press (1997)

9 8 7 6 5 4 3 2 1

A catalogue record for this book is available from the British Library.

Typesetting: Marie Doherty
Illustrations: Louis Mackay
Printed in the UK by TJ International Ltd.

Contents

Introduction: The unexamined risk — 1

Chapter 1: The five key principles of crisis management — 15

Chapter 2: What's in my burger? — 39

Chapter 3: Says who? Extraterritorial legislation — 69

Chapter 4: Rogue employees: The threat from within — 91

Chapter 5: The rock and the whirlpool — 123

Chapter 6: NGOs and organisational activism — 149

Chapter 7: The cyber threat — 169

Conclusion — 195

Notes — 199
Index — 203

Introduction

The unexamined risk

YOU CAN'T HELP BUT FEEL A BIT SORRY FOR TONY HAYWARD. WHEN HE joined BP as a young geologist in 1982, the thought of one day becoming CEO of one of the world's top ten companies must have seemed like a distant pipe dream. He spent his whole career working his way up the corporate ladder and finally the dream came true. In May 2007, he was appointed CEO. Then, two years later when the *Deepwater Horizon* rig exploded in the Gulf of Mexico, the dream became a nightmare. Within five months, he was out of a job.

BP was Tony Hayward's life. He met his wife, Maureen Fulton, at BP while she was working there as a geophysicist. He travelled the world on expatriate assignments for the oil major, living in a wide range of countries including China, Vietnam, Mongolia, Colombia and Venezuela. His seven years in Latin America had an impact on his personality and he 'learned to think with [his] heart and not just [his] head'.[1] When he finally took over from Lord Browne as CEO, he was keen to demonstrate a change in style. Where Lord Browne, nicknamed the 'Sun King', had run BP with an imperious, dictatorial style, Tony Hayward wanted to introduce a more collegiate atmosphere. He turned his predecessor's palatial suite of offices into meeting rooms and moved into something smaller and more modest. Out went the expensive art collection, replaced by low-key photographs of his family and his hobby, sailing.

Tony Hayward's style was relaxed and down to earth; he had a boyish enthusiasm and a smile that was almost cherubic. He had a team approach to management, listening to opinions and trying to find a group consensus. He spoke in a straightforward way. His responses were often unguarded, informal and passionate. The stereotypical CEO is an egotistical monster, surrounded by a fawning court of 'yes' men, living in a bubble of complacent narcissism and mouthing a stream of bland pre-processed cant. Tony Hayward was the opposite: a CEO who was *almost* human. Sadly, this was the root cause of his subsequent downfall.

The *Deepwater Horizon* was a drilling rig, built in South Korea, owned by Swiss-based Transocean, and registered under a Marshall Islands flag of convenience to reduce operating costs. In February 2010, it was chartered by BP at a cost of $96 million to spend a month drilling a 10-km-deep exploratory well in the Macondo prospect in the Gulf of Mexico, 66 km off the coast of Louisiana. Drilling actually took two months and the well was finally completed in April. The wellhead was cemented over by the subcontractor, Halliburton, blocking it off until another specialised rig could be brought in at a later date to begin extracting the oil. On 20 April, several BP managers gathered together on the *Deepwater Horizon* to conduct a short ceremony to celebrate seven years without an injury on that rig. With the cruellest of ironies, at 9.45 p.m. that same day a blast of methane gas came shooting up the wellbore onto the deck of the rig, triggering a huge explosion that killed 11 workers and injured a further 17. The fire raged for another two days before the whole rig sank beneath the waves on 22 April, which, in another ironic coincidence, happened to be Earth Day.

What followed was a PR nightmare. For 87 days, in the inky silence of the ocean, 1.5 km below the surface, the well spewed forth its noxious plume of oil. Above the surface, it was all colour, sound and fury. TV screens worldwide were filled with pictures of oil-covered pelicans, beaches befouled with tar, dead baby dolphins washed up on the shoreline and trusty, local fishermen bemoaning the loss of their livelihoods.

Efforts to cap the well traced an arc of heroic failures that could have been scripted in Hollywood. First, BP tried remotely controlled submersible robots, which failed. Then it tried deploying a containment dome, a massive inverted funnel that could gather and direct the oil safely to the surface, but this became blocked by gas crystals in the intense cold. Then came a succession of improbably named fixes like the 'Top Kill' and 'Top Hat Number 10'. They also failed.

For environmentalists, the proposed remedies were almost worse than the disease. They included extensive spraying with toxic chemicals to disperse the slicks and releasing genetically modified microbes into the ocean to digest the surplus oil. It was even suggested that a nuclear bomb could be used to permanently seal the well. In the end, a second relief well had to be drilled to relieve the pressure. This then allowed cement to be pumped into the original hole, sealing it off. Finally on 19 September, the well was effectively plugged, stopping the oil spill for good.

The causes of the accident were the subject of much acrimonious debate and finger pointing. Was Halliburton to blame for doing a faulty cement job? What about the blowout preventer, which manifestly failed – a device designed specifically to avoid this type of accident, and built by Cameron International Corp? What about Transocean? It owned the rig and it was Transocean engineers who replaced the drilling fluid with seawater that was insufficiently dense to contain the methane gas. The court cases to apportion liability for the disaster are still rumbling on today. At the time, and in the mind of the American public, there was only one villain in the piece – BP – and sitting at its head was Tony Hayward.

Drilling for oil offshore is a risky business. The last major disaster had been the explosion on the *Piper Alpha* platform in the North Sea in 1988, which killed 167 rig workers. In that case, in a neat reversal of the *Deepwater Horizon* episode, it had been a US oil company, Occidental, drilling in UK territorial waters. Two days after the accident, Arnold Hammer, the chairman of Occidental, had tea with Prime

Minister Margaret Thatcher. They then stood together on the steps of Number 10 while the prime minister told the press 'what a wonderful man' Hammer was.[2] The press was full of sympathy for the victims and their families and admiration for the derring-do of Red Adair, the Texan firefighter who eventually put out the blaze.

Twenty-five years later, when Tony Hayward was in the hot seat, that was not the way it played out at all. No cosy chats with President Obama for him. Instead, Obama was open and scathing in his criticism of BP's CEO. The public mood was uniformly hostile and the president, recalling George W. Bush's Hurricane Katrina fiasco, was keen to appear on top of the crisis and to bash whatever scapegoat was to hand. If it was a foreign multinational, then so much the better.

Tony Hayward made an easy target and a series of PR gaffes just made his situation worse. One of the first comments he made to the press was, 'The Gulf of Mexico is a very big ocean. The volume of oil and dispersant we are putting into it is tiny in relation to the total water volume'.[3] A sensible, measured, top-down view and one that was scientifically correct, but it was completely at odds with the public mood. In the same interview, he was asked if he thought his job was on the line. He replied, 'I will be judged by the nature of my response.'

Judged he was. A week later, he was forced to revise his opinion, telling CNN that the oil spill was 'an environmental catastrophe'. Soon after, in a TV interview on 30 May, he tried to express his empathy with the victims of the oil spill: 'We're sorry for the massive disruption it's caused to their lives. There's no one who wants this thing over more than I do; I'd like my life back.' It was an unguarded comment in which he was trying to express his emotional involvement with the crisis. It was also a PR disaster. He was roundly condemned for appearing selfish; what about the lives of the people who had died in the explosion? From then on, it just got worse. Grilled by a Congressional hearing, he appeared evasive and unco-operative. He read from a prepared statement and often replied 'I can't recall' or 'I can't answer that question'. Taking his only day off after two months of extreme stress, he was then photographed on his yacht sailing in a race around the Isle of Wight, which made him appear aloof and uncaring. It was all getting to be too much. On 23 July 2010, BP issued a statement declaring that Tony Hayward had the full support of the board,[4] but five days later they had changed their minds and announced that Bob Dudley would take over as CEO.

That's the way it all ended for Tony: first with a bang and *then* with a whimper.* He was a decent man caught up in a corporate crisis not of his own making, and whose reaction to it was probably similar to what you or I would have done in his shoes. It was a crisis that came as a *Bolt from the Blue*.

This book is about corporate crises; where they come from, what form they take and what you can do about them. There are plenty of useful lessons to be learned, as we will show through examining various case studies. They all start the same way, though – with a cloud on the horizon, at first no bigger than a man's hand, which soon transforms into a deadly tempest. In BP's case it was not, strictly speaking, deadly in a corporate sense. The company survived and Tony Hayward soon got another job in the oil business running Genel Energy, an adventurous start-up with operations in northern Iraq.

The next crisis we will look at *did* prove to be deadly. Enron was founded in 1985 when Kenneth Lay merged two Texan gas utilities: Houston Natural Gas and InterNorth. The deregulation of the gas sector created a new market for energy trading, which Enron enthusiastically embraced. Where previously gas had been sold through long-term fixed contracts between suppliers and consumers, the newly deregulated energy markets allowed middlemen like Enron to trade contracts on a short-term basis, which allowed better price discovery and more efficient matching between supply and demand. It also ushered in a host of new financial instruments to hedge against future price fluctuations. As a result, the gas utility sector, famously a shrine for

---

* Apologies to T.S. Eliot for the misquotation.

the staid and the stolid, was injected with a shot of casino hocus pocus and brokers' brio. At the forefront of this transformation was Enron.

Revenues skyrocketed. In 1996, Enron's revenues totalled $13 billion. In just four years they increased more than tenfold, to $140 billion, taking Enron to number 6 in the Fortune Global 500 in 2001. The company was showered with praise; it was a darling of the stock analysts on Wall Street and *Fortune* magazine named it 'America's Most Innovative Company' for six years in a row. Such stellar growth seemed almost too good to be true. In fact, it was. But Enron was aggressive in defending its reputation, bullying analysts and journalists who dared to criticise it so that no one dared to question whether the emperor actually had any clothes. It was only later, when the company declared bankruptcy in December 2001, that the truth came out: the company's accounts were a complete fiction.

The two main pillars of any set of accounts are the balance sheet and the profit and loss account (P&L). The point of this 'stereoscopic' view, a static snapshot of assets and an annual summary of profits, is that it gives a complete description of the state of the company. There is nowhere to hide. Changes in one can be tracked through the cash flow statement to an impact on the other. But in Enron's case, both the balance sheet and the P&L account were such elaborate confections that even a Parisian patissier would have been proud.

The first way in which Enron distorted its accounts was in the recognition of revenue. When a manufacturer sells a widget, the value of the widget is booked as revenue and the costs such as raw material and labour are subtracted to determine the profit. It is different for service companies; someone acting as a broker or middleman only books the agency fee as revenue. Let's say an estate agent sells you a house for £1 million,* on which he earns a fee of 3 per cent, or £30,000. The normal practice would be to book the £30,000 as revenue, not the total value of the transaction of £1 million. However, Enron was booking

---

* If you aren't wealthy enough yet to afford a house at this price, dear reader, then we fervently hope you soon will be...

the total value of the transaction as revenue, not just the fee, which is why its revenues looked so enormous. Had it used normal accounting practice, its revenues would have been something like $7 billion in 2001 rather than $140 billion, a fairly sizeable difference.

The second distorting trick on the P&L was to use 'mark-to-market' accounting. Normal accounting practice is to recognise revenue after a service has been provided and the cash has either been collected or is about to be in the very near future. Mark-to-market accounting deviates from this principle. Let's say Enron sold a ten-year fixed-price contract for gas to a customer and then immediately went into the derivatives market and hedged his exposure, thereby locking in his profit. Enron then held two contracts, one for the customer and one for the derivatives, which 'guaranteed' a stream of profits over the next ten years. In theory, it did not matter if the gas price fluctuated during that period since the derivatives contract would compensate for any losses on the customer contract and vice versa; the risk was hedged. Enron argued that the future revenue stream on the deal, cooked up in five minutes on the trading desk, should be recognised *now* rather than gradually over the next ten years. Once this principle was established, Enron was free to make its revenue figures whatever it felt like. Since the only people who knew how to value these complex derivative structures were the traders who were selling them, it was a licence to cook the books at will.

The balance sheet was an even greater work of fiction. The CFO, Andrew Fastow, created a confusing array of special purpose entities with lurid names such as Jedi, Chewco and Raptor V. These looked like they were legitimate third-party entities but were in fact controlled by Fastow, who even had the gall to collect a personal fee for setting them up. With these special purpose entities in place, massaging the balance sheet was simple. Assets and liabilities could be shuffled between Enron and these other vehicles whenever was convenient. When an asset was sold, Enron was effectively buying it from itself at whatever price Fastow cared to invent.

The problem with cooking the books is that, once you start, you have to continue. Next year's figures need to look better than last year's, so you cheat a little bit more. This went on for a six-year period until the bubble finally burst. Enron filed for bankruptcy and the fraudulent activity of the senior management was exposed for the entire world to see. Kenneth Lay, the CEO, had been selling his Enron stock heavily in the months before the bankruptcy and managed to net himself $20 million in proceeds while at the same time reassuring the outside world that all was fine. The poor employees, all 17,000 of them, saw their pensions wiped out as their pension fund was fully invested in Enron stock that proved to be worthless. The disgust the public felt at the CEO's behaviour was best expressed by Senator Byron Dorgan in a Senate Committee Hearing into the scandal:

> In the *Titanic*, the captain went down with the ship. And Enron looks to me like the captain first gave himself and his friends a bonus, then lowered himself and the top folks down [into] the lifeboat and then hollered up and said, 'By the way, everything is going to be just fine.'

This book is about unexpected crises. For the senior management at Enron, the bankruptcy did not come as a surprise. They had been deliberately, carefully and systematically defrauding the public for a number of years and must have known that they would be found out in the end. So the moral of this story is not really focused on Enron but instead concerns another company, a well-regarded pillar of the corporate landscape for whom the Enron bankruptcy was a fatal blow. For this company, the Enron scandal was a crisis that *did* come 'out of the blue'. The crisis ended abruptly its proud 90-year history. The company was Arthur Andersen.

Arthur E. Andersen founded his eponymous accounting firm in 1913, just before the First World War. Orphaned at 16, he put himself through night school by working as a mailboy and became a certified accountant. The core values that he demonstrated at this young age were embedded in the firm that he founded: rectitude, discipline, honesty, hard work and attention to detail. He ran the firm until his death in 1947 and held one particular principle to be of paramount importance: the customer is *not* always right. Andersen believed the prime responsibility of the accountant was to the investor and not to the client who was paying for the service. When faced with the choice between signing off on a misleading set of accounts or losing a major client, he always picked the latter. Several high-profile clients were shown the door during his reign. The governing mantra was probity before profits.

All this began to change in the 1970s with the growth in Arthur Andersen's consulting business. Giving advice to companies was far more lucrative than balancing their ledgers; management consultants could charge much higher day rates than accountants. To begin with, the new division focused on advice about IT systems but soon broadened into all areas of management consultancy so that, by the 1990s, the bulk of the firm's revenues came from giving advice, with the traditional audit partners seen as the poor relations.

The difference in culture between the two sides of the business was the cause of much friction. A consultant, in a popular aphorism, is a man who borrows your watch to tell you the time. Companies often hire consultants not because they don't know what to do, but because they have already decided what to do and want an external third party to ratify it. A cynic would say a management consultant is there to tell the client what they want to hear and the more they charge, the better that 'independent' advice is. This is in complete opposition to the role of an auditor who is certifying to the general public that the company's books are kosher. A consultant is there to develop management's vision; an auditor is there to challenge it. Slowly, as the consulting side became more and more successful, values became eroded and the founding culture undone.

Relations between the two sides of Andersen's business became increasingly acrimonious, leading to a split in January 2001, when

Andersen Consulting renamed itself Accenture. But the damage was already done. Within nine months, Andersen found itself at the centre of the Enron scandal. David Duncan, the audit partner who had run the Enron account since 1997, ordered his staff to start shredding thousands of documents and deleting emails related to Enron. He was fired by Andersen in January 2012. But if the accounting firm hoped to make him a scapegoat, this strategy backfired when Duncan plea-bargained his way into becoming the star witness for the prosecution. Chapter 4 on rogue employees examines the dangers of adopting a 'scapegoat' strategy in more detail. Once the details of Enron's fraudulent behaviour and the fictitious nature of its accounts became public, Andersen's reputation was completely destroyed. Arthur Andersen surrendered its CPA licence on 31 August 2002, meaning it could no longer sign off public accounts and therefore could no longer operate. At a stroke, 85,000 employees lost their jobs; one rogue partner colluding with a fraudulent client had just destroyed a highly respected part of the American corporate establishment.

Honest accounting is a key foundation stone of the whole edifice of capitalism in the West. These foundations had been badly shaken by the Enron scandal and the implosion of Arthur Andersen. The public was scandalised and a regulatory response was swift in coming. The Public Company Accounting Reform and Investor Protection Act was passed by the US Senate in July 2002, better known as the Sarbanes–Oxley Act, or SOX for short. The Act aimed to improve the veracity of corporate financial statements; it also introduced stricter penalties for fraudulent financial activity and the requirement that senior management personally sign off on the accuracy of their financial statements.

To some, this regulatory cure was worse than the disease. As is often the case with regulation, a well-intentioned law has unintended consequences. As a result, the regulatory burden increases but the problem still is not fixed. Fairly soon, new legislation is required to deal with the consequences of the first Act and the cycle begins again in an ever-increasing spiral of red tape. So it proved in this case. Eight years after Sarbanes–Oxley, an even more weighty corpus of legislation, the Dodd–Frank Act, was passed by Congress in a further attempt to improve accountability and transparency in the corporate world, stem fraud and protect investors.

The *Wall Street Journal* has been particularly critical of the Sarbanes–Oxley Act. In an editorial on 21 December 2008 it stated, 'The new laws and regulations have neither prevented frauds nor instituted fairness. But they have managed to kill the creation of new public companies in the U.S., cripple the venture capital business, and damage entrepreneurship.' More recently, on 4 January 2012, it returned to this theme in another editorial, stating:

> For the third year in a row the world's leading exchange for new stock offerings was located not in New York, but in Hong Kong. . . . Given that the U.S. is still home to the world's largest economy, there's no reason it shouldn't have the most vibrant equity markets – unless regulation is holding back the creation of new public companies. On that score it's getting harder for backers of the Sarbanes–Oxley accounting law to explain away each disappointing year since its 2002 enactment as some kind of temporary or unrelated setback.

America likes to see itself as the 'land of the free' but in fact is one of the most regulated societies on earth. If 'freedom' is interpreted to mean the freedom to do anything you like without regulations getting in the way, then the best candidate for the soubriquet of 'land of the free' is probably Somalia. In a similar vein, if regulation is intended to reduce risk, from a corporate perspective it often actually increases it. The conventional view is that emerging markets have fast-growing economies but are 'riskier' than traditional markets in the developed world. In fact, it is the risk in the developed world – the risk presented by the regulatory regime – that is most overlooked or underestimated. Regulatory risk is often the unexamined risk.

Look at the case of JPMorgan. When rumours of massive losses run up by a rogue trader dubbed the 'London Whale' first came to light in April 2012, JPMorgan's CEO, Jamie Dimon, dismissed them as 'a storm in a teacup'. This denial was soon followed by shame-faced acceptance when Dimon admitted a month later that the bank's trading strategy had been 'flawed, complex, poorly reviewed, poorly executed and poorly monitored'[5] and had cost the bank more than $2 billion in mark-to-market losses. Even worse, these huge unauthorised positions on the London trading desk had breached compliance rules and the bank ultimately had to pay $920 million in fines to regulators including the Securities and Exchange Commission (SEC) in the US and the Financial Conduct Authority (FCA) in the UK. It also added 4,000 new compliance staff to make sure it stayed on the right side of the rules in future. Clearly, the risk is no longer just that a trader goes rogue and loses a stack of money. The regulatory regime itself is a risk; a peril on your home turf that can prove much more costly than an unsuccessful foray into a frontier market on the other side of the world.

In this book, we aim to look at all the different cardinal points of corporate risk in turn, as illustrated in Figure 1. The risk domain can be described by two axes: internal versus external and public sector versus private sector. Using this delineation, we can work our way around the compass of corporate risk, chapter by chapter. Chapter 2 is concerned with supply chain risk, whereby your organisation is required to carry the can for a subcontractor that has let it down. In Chapter 3, we look at regulatory risk, with an emphasis on extraterritoriality – the application of rules outside their national boundaries. For a multinational, it is no longer enough to follow the aphorism 'when in Rome, do as the Romans do'. Now you need to 'do as the Romans do' even when you are not in Rome. In Chapter 4, we examine the way in which public opinion drives the introduction of new regulation and the difficulties of navigating between the rock of legislation and the whirlpool of the *vox populi* (voice of the people). Many companies find themselves caught in this vice between two forces over which they have little control: the

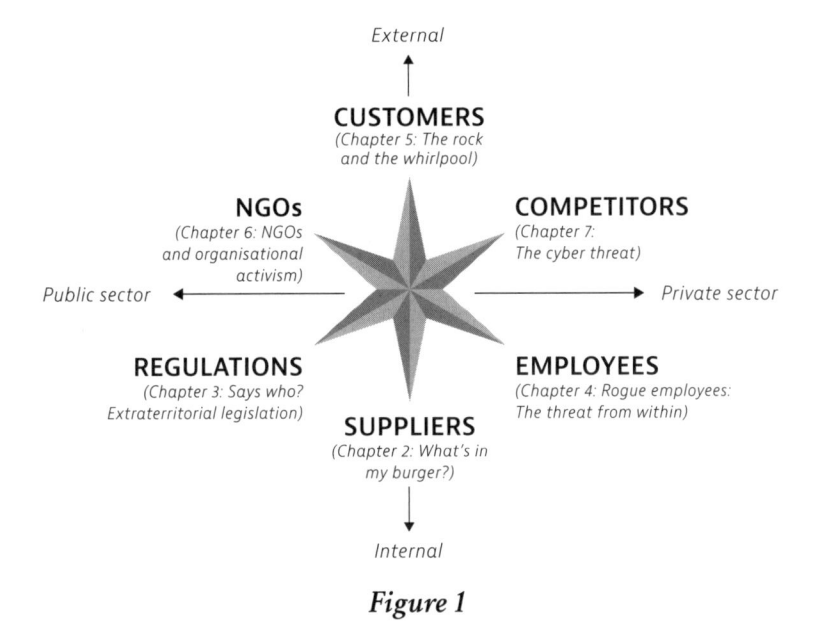

```
                    External
                       ↑
                  CUSTOMERS
                 (Chapter 5: The rock
                  and the whirlpool)
         NGOs                    COMPETITORS
   (Chapter 6: NGOs              (Chapter 7:
   and organisational            The cyber threat)
       activism)
Public sector  ←────────★────────→  Private sector
       REGULATIONS              EMPLOYEES
     (Chapter 3: Says who?      (Chapter 4: Rogue employees:
    Extraterritorial legislation)  The threat from within)
                  SUPPLIERS
                 (Chapter 2: What's in
                   my burger?)
                       ↓
                    Internal
```

Figure 1

rational world of the law courts and the emotive world of the court of public opinion. Chapter 5 focuses on risks inside the organisation in the form of rogue employees and whistleblowers. As the Arthur Andersen example shows, trying to scapegoat an individual in a crisis, even if he truly was solely culpable, rarely works nowadays. Those at the top are deemed responsible for every deck of the ship. Chapter 6 looks at the external threat presented by non-governmental organisations (NGOs) and Chapter 7 is all about the risks posed by cyber attack. But before all of that, in Chapter 1, we look at the key principles of crisis management. In the various crises faced by BP, Enron, Arthur Andersen and JPMorgan described above, some common mistakes were made from which some broad conclusions can be drawn about how to manage a corporate crisis. It is to this topic that we now turn.

CHAPTER 1

The five key principles of crisis management

> When war does come, my advice is to draw
> the sword and throw away the scabbard.
>
> *General 'Stonewall' Jackson, speech to cadets at*
> *the Virginia Military Institute, March 1861*

IT IS OFTEN SAID THAT 'GENERALS ALWAYS FIGHT THE LAST WAR'. THIS IS because they spend most of peacetime studying history and developing tactics for known threats. However, advances in technology change the nature of the battlefield. This means that their plans are generally obsolete from the moment a new war starts. No plan survives first contact with the enemy, as German General Helmuth von Moltke famously said.

The massed cavalry charge, which was so devastatingly effective in the Napoleonic era, became suicidal in the American Civil War. Smoothbore muskets had been replaced by rifles, which had a much longer range and could cut down a cavalry charge with ease. As a result, the cavalry spent most of their time dismounting and fighting on foot like infantry. These tactics were, in turn, undermined 50 years later as technology further developed.

The vulnerability of infantry was demonstrated in the First World War. Machine guns and fortified trenches gave defenders an overwhelming advantage. Advancing infantry was mown down like reaped wheat in the crossfire from the opposing trenches. The overwhelming strength of fortified defences was a lesson learnt at appalling expense, and paid for with the lives of millions of foot soldiers. French military planners, having learnt this lesson, built the Maginot Line in the 1930s: an impenetrable string of concrete fortifications and interconnected bunkers that ran the length of the Franco–German border. Unfortunately, it was trounced by Germany's 'blitzkrieg' tactics in the Second World War. German panzer divisions simply went around the end of the Maginot Line through the Ardennes and Belgium. So, despite this impenetrable wall, France fell within six weeks. This was an inconceivable outcome to any soldier who had spent the First World War engaged in static trench warfare, just one generation previously.

Generals always fight the last war. At school my beleaguered history teacher, faced with an unruly class, would often quote an even more timeworn adage: 'those who do not study history are condemned to repeat their mistakes'. But it seems that those who *do* study history are *also* condemned to making mistakes, particularly when a war or crisis looms. It's not just generals who make this error. Several years on from the financial crisis of 2007, economic growth in the West is far from robust (particularly in Europe) despite interest rates being held at unprecedentedly low levels for an extraordinarily long period. This situation prompts many commentators to quip that 'economists are fighting the last depression'. Through quantitative easing, central banks have flooded the market with cheap money by buying back government bonds. High interest rates were seen as the cause of the Great Depression of the 1930s. Central bankers, having studied history, have floored interest rates with unprecedented vigour but it doesn't seem to be working. They may well be fighting the previous war.

As with generals and economists, so with corporate risk management. Every major company has a contingency plan in its bottom drawer to deal with a crisis such as the kidnapping of the CEO. It is sitting there, prepared in exhaustive detail by the business continuity and corporate security departments, ready to be pulled out at a moment's notice. But the last time a CEO was kidnapped was in the mid 1970s. Technology has changed and risks have moved on since then. How many companies have a cyber security plan? Given the magnitude of this type of threat, the answer is – not enough. The death of a CEO, though tragic, is not fatal for the organisation. There is always a new CEO waiting in the wings. In contrast, the theft of critical intellectual property in a cyber attack could be a far more serious blow.

Ignoramus et ignorabimus

At a press briefing on 12 February 2002, the US Secretary of Defense Donald Rumsfeld was addressing the absence of evidence of weapons of mass destruction (WMDs) in Iraq. He offered the following argument in support of his decision to go to war:

> Reports that say that something hasn't happened are always interesting to me, because as we know, there are known knowns; there are things we know we know. We also know there are known unknowns; that is to say, we know there are some things we do not know. But there are also unknown unknowns – the ones we don't know we don't know.

This tortured and convoluted language is reminiscent of the muscular writhings of an octopus in a confined space; not unlike the tight spot that Rumsfeld found himself in. It prompted much hilarity and ridicule in the press and he was awarded the 2003 Foot in Mouth award as a result. But the point he was trying to make is both valid and important. It is more pithily summarised in the Latin phrase 'ignoramus et ignorabimus', meaning 'we do not know and we can not know'.

A CEO never knows where the next crisis is coming from. Crises always come out of the blue, which is a tautological statement because it is its very unexpectedness that makes a crisis a crisis. So there can be plenty of contingency plans in the bottom drawer dealing with the 'known knowns' or even the 'known unknowns' but the crisis will blow in from the third area: the 'unknown unknowns' – the event that there is no plan for. In fact, an even more dangerous fourth area exists, which Rumsfeld overlooked. In order to untangle the writhing octopus, however, we need to express it in a different way.

The word 'unknown', used in this context, can mean two things: either that the observer is unaware of an event or that a particular outcome is unpredictable. So we can recast Rumsfeld's statement using the two concepts of 'predictability' and 'awareness', as illustrated in Figure 2.

In the first quadrant are the 'known knowns'. These are issues that a CEO is aware of and whose outcomes are fairly predictable. This is the quadrant where business planning is most effective and is the normal focus of management attention. A good example is next

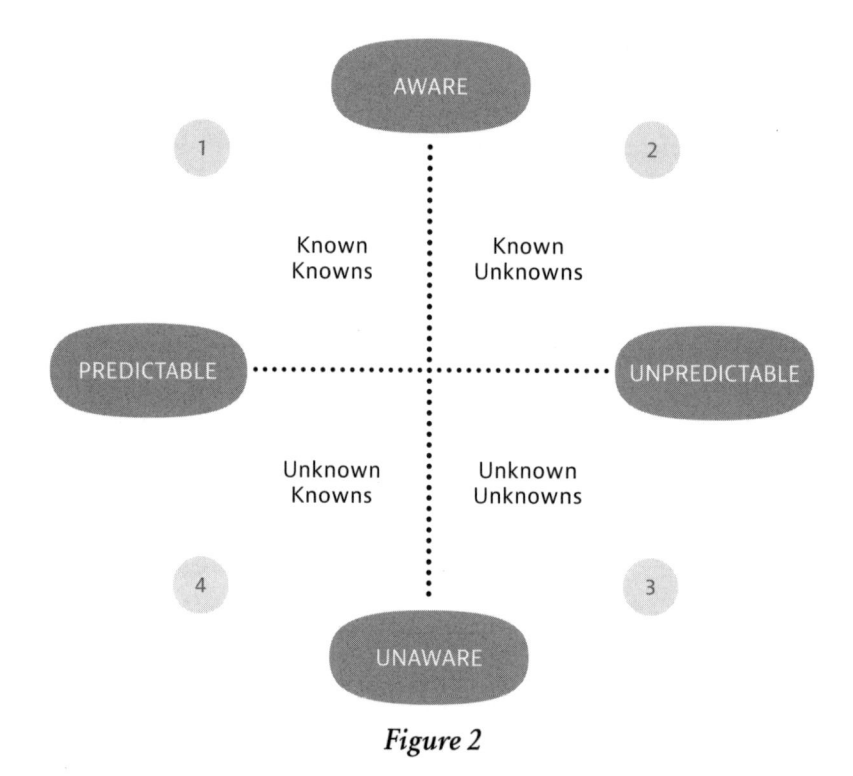

	AWARE	
1	Known Knowns : Known Unknowns	2
PREDICTABLE	....	UNPREDICTABLE
4	Unknown Knowns : Unknown Unknowns	3
	UNAWARE	

Figure 2

quarter's revenue figures. Although some uncertainty always exists, most companies can predict these figures with a reasonable degree of accuracy. The issues affecting the outcome are fairly well known: new product launches, consumer demand forecasts, advertising budgets, the strength of competitors, major new customers on the horizon and marketing incentives are all somewhere in the mix. These factors are both well understood by management and fairly predictable and so can be modelled in a spreadsheet to produce a plausible forecast.

The second quadrant, 'known unknowns', contains issues of which management is aware but that are inherently unpredictable. Examples include the risk of a catastrophic flood, a kidnapping, a terrorist attack, an earthquake destroying a key subcontractor's facility or a coup in a foreign country. These types of risk are quite binary. The likelihood of them occurring is very low but if they did happen they would cause major disruptions. These issues would not normally be factored into a model forecasting future revenues. Rather, they would be addressed by business continuity planning. Risks are clearly higher here, but can be mitigated to some extent by examining a number of possible outcomes and conducting sensitivity analysis for each potential issue. In this way, some of the darkness of uncertainty can be partially illuminated.

The third quadrant, 'unknown unknowns', contains issues that no one has even thought of yet. They are not just unpredictable but, to make matters worse, no one is even aware of them. It is the third quadrant that Rumsfeld was trying to focus the media's attention on. His argument was that, even though it was uncertain whether or not Saddam Hussein had WMDs, the risk warranted the decision to go to war. Invasion of Iraq was justified by the 'unknown unknowns'; in other words, the threats of an unspecified nature that are not even suspected to be there.

A moment's reflection will show that this is a pretty flimsy argument. First, since WMDs were actually specified, this must surely be a known threat: it belongs in the second quadrant not the third. Second, an 'unspecified and unknowable' threat is surely the opposite of justification because the latter implies a set of facts both specified and known. Put the other way round, the third quadrant in Rumsfeld's logic could be used to invade any country in the world at whim, which may well have been his intention.

It is the neatest of ironies that Rumsfeld was undone by events in the fourth quadrant; the quadrant he did not even recognise or mention. These are the 'unknown knowns': facts that are known at some lower level in the organisation but of which the CEO is unaware. It was the scandal caused by the torture and abuse of prisoners in Abu Ghraib that led to his resignation. How fitting that the cause of his demise occurred in the place he least expected it – not among the 'unknowns' but among the 'knowns' he had overlooked.

RULE 1. *Do not deny anything before you are in full possession of the facts*

From a CEO's perspective, the fourth quadrant is the most dangerous. Though the crisis will enter in the third quadrant, it is in the fourth quadrant that most damage will occur. The natural and most instinctive response to a crisis is denial, usually before the full facts have been established. When facts subsequently emerge that contradict the CEO's initial statements, that CEO is dead meat. The general public will normally forgive an unforeseen event, but they will not forgive a cover-up. So for a CEO to deny things before they are in full possession of the facts is extremely dangerous. The first response in a crisis should always be to investigate the 'unknown knowns': what facts are known at a lower level in the organisation of which the CEO is unaware? What have the divisional managers and subordinates been hiding from them?

The egg cup and the pea

You will notice in the above diagram that the two axes have a key distinguishing factor. The 'awareness' axis lies inside management control while the 'predictability' axis does not. A CEO can always make themself more aware of the facts through better internal communications, red-flagging protocols and more thorough management reporting. However, this is not the case with the 'predictability' axis because, as Danish physicist Niels Bohr once wryly observed, 'prediction is difficult, especially about the future'. The problem is compounded when you are dealing with a 'non-linear' system.

Most of the mathematical tools in common usage are linear in nature; in other words, the output is predictably proportional to the input. So for a simple equation like $y = 3x + 1$, once you know the input (x), you can calculate the output (y) by multiplying by three and adding one. This holds true regardless of whether the value of x – the input – is six or a million. In a linear system, the initial conditions are unimportant.

Everything you learn on an MBA course is based on linear mathematics, including accounting, probability theory, demand modelling, optimal pricing, profit forecasting and investment analysis. Unfortunately, the real world is non-linear. Here, initial conditions are very important and outcomes are unpredictable. The best way to illustrate this concept is to imagine a dried pea sitting at the bottom of an egg cup. This is an inherently stable linear system. If you randomly knock the pea in any direction, it will rattle around a bit but ultimately end up back at the bottom of the egg cup exactly where it started. Even though a bit of randomness occurs at the beginning, it is quite easy to predict the final outcome. Now imagine that you turn the egg cup upside down and carefully balance the pea on top. This is an inherently unstable, non-linear system. If you randomly knock the pea in any direction, it will roll down the side of the egg cup, bounce across the table, fall onto the floor and end up in the far corner of the room. The chance of you being able to predict where the pea will land is almost zero. A slight randomness in the input leads to an unpredictably wide range of possible outcomes. The pea inside the egg cup is on the left-hand side of the diagram (quadrants 1 and 4) ; the pea balanced on top of the egg cup is on the right-hand side (quadrants 2 and 3).

To use a slightly more complicated analogy, think of a game of billiards. In order to knock the black ball into the pocket, you must strike the cue ball so that it moves in a particular direction at a particular speed. You could theoretically calculate the correct angles and momentums involved using Newton's laws, although, of course, a skilled player is doing precisely that instinctively by eye. The point is that a game of billiards is a linear system. Once you know the direction and speed of the cue ball, everything else is predictable. It is also repeatable. If, sometime later, you put all the balls back in exactly the same positions and played precisely the same shots, the outcome would be the same.

A non-linear system is a billiard table on a yacht. As the boat is gently rocked by the waves, the billiard table tilts in an unpredictable way. The shot you play is now very dependent on the initial conditions; are you playing slightly uphill or downhill? It is no longer predictable or repeatable. You have to take account of the slight slope on the table at the exact moment you strike the ball. Let's compound the difficulty by supposing that the billiard table is not flat. Imagine the green baize covering an undulating landscape of shallow bumps and valleys. That is yet another complex environmental factor to take into account. The system is now so complicated that the only way to guarantee that the ball will end up in the desired place is to steer it there by continuously pushing it across the table.

By steering the ball across the table rather than just striking it once, you have introduced a control mechanism. The only way to get the required outcome from an unpredictable, non-linear system is by establishing continuous control based on some sort of feedback mechanism. That knowledge will not come as a surprise to any pragmatic CEO. It's just a long-winded way of saying that complex systems, like companies, need steering to get the right results. Sometimes, in fair weather, only a light touch now and again on the tiller is needed. But, in heavy weather, steering the right course requires constant attention, making manual adjustments moment by moment in response to local conditions. That, in engineering terms, is what is meant by a feedback control loop.

A control system driven by 'active feedback' means that the output is connected in some way to the input. The output from the system is monitored and used to amplify or attenuate the input. The best example is the high-pitched yowl from a live mic on stage. The microphone is picking up the sound coming from the speakers and passing it to the amplifier, which then pumps it out to the speakers again, so completing the feedback circuit. The result is an ever-increasing spiral of amplified white noise, which you hear as a high-pitched atonal screeching (of course, at a heavy metal concert, that's the lead singer and he is supposed to sound like that).

Microphone feedback is an unintended error, but feedback is normally a beneficial process and vitally important for controlling complex, non-linear systems. Cruise control in a car is a good example. If you want your car to travel at a constant speed, the simplest solution is to hold the throttle in a fixed position. The problem is that, when you start to go up a hill, the car will slow down. So a better solution is to constantly monitor the speed of the car and then adjust the throttle to keep the speed constant; opening it when going up a hill and closing it when going down. This is what a cruise control system does. The output (the speed of the car) is used to control the input (the throttle) through a feedback loop. Of course, anyone actually driving a car without cruise control uses the throttle in this way automatically, without even thinking about it; the active feedback controller is the driver themself.

You may be wondering by now whether this lengthy technical discussion about active feedback loops has a point since the conclusions so far seem fairly banal. But there is a key engineering principle at the heart of control theory that has important implications for crisis management. It concerns the controllability of the system and can be easily demonstrated with a simple practical experiment.

For this experiment you need a pencil and a long-handled broom. Try balancing a pencil on the end of one finger. You will find it almost impossible. Within less than a second it will have fallen off. Now try with the broom. If you can, remove the brush from the end and just use

24 *Bolt from the Blue*

It is easy to balance a broomstick on the end of your finger ...

... but almost impossible to do it with a pencil

Try it!

What does that teach you about crisis management?

the broomstick. After a bit of practice, you should find it quite easy to do for more than ten seconds or so.

So why is it easy to balance a big heavy object like a broomstick on the end of your finger but almost impossible to do so with a much smaller object like a pencil? The answer is to do with the speed of the feedback loop. As when driving a car without cruise control, the feedback control in this case is provided by you. You are monitoring the output by watching the stick with your eyes. You are then feeding the information back to the input by moving your finger to keep it balanced. A heavy broomstick has more inertia and therefore moves more slowly than a light pencil. In essence, you can control the broomstick because it moves more slowly than the pencil.

For a system to be controllable, the speed of the feedback loop must be faster than the speed of the system. This makes intuitive sense. If your 'correction' messages are not getting through fast enough, the system will spin out of control. Your corrections will make the system less stable rather than more stable because they are out of date. The speed of the feedback loop in this case is your reaction time. As soon as the object is smaller than a certain size, you will lose the ability to control it.

So what lessons can we draw from these analogies to use in managing a crisis? A crisis is a great example of a non-linear system. So to manage it we need a feedback-based control system. We need to closely monitor the outcome of our actions and use that to change our strategy at input. What is more, for the crisis to be controllable, the speed of our reaction time needs to be faster than the speed of the story.

RULE 2. *Your response time must be faster than the speed of the story*

Responding to a crisis faster than the story describing it has become increasingly difficult in the light of new technology. The speed at which a story travels is getting faster and faster. A generation ago, when the main delivery mechanism for news was printed newspapers, stories had a diurnal rhythm and news followed a daily cycle. The advent of 24-hour TV news channels such as CNN shrank that to an hourly cycle. The social media revolution has reduced that time even further; Twitter, Facebook and blogs enable news stories to travel at an unprecedented speed.

The heavy broomstick has more inertia than the pencil and therefore moves more slowly. Inside a large organisation it is bureaucratic inertia that slows things down. So, in a sense, bureaucracy is the enemy of crisis management because it slows down response times. This may seem contradictory because a bureaucracy is expressly designed to deal with problems: to neuter the unexpected through a series of policies and procedures and transmute it into the norm.

Bureaucracy functions like the egg cup containing the pea. It can cope with random perturbations by gently but firmly steering the pea back towards the status quo at the bottom of the cup. The inherent checks and balances of a bureaucratic system act to restore order. But, in a crisis, the egg cup is turned upside down and the pea shoots out. In a crisis, the existing bureaucracy is part of the problem. To find out why, it is worth spending a little time exploring the strengths and weaknesses inherent in a corporate bureaucracy.

The nature of bureaucracy

As I sit writing these words, my eyes are distracted by something glinting near the window to my right. The low rays of the evening sun are shining through a blue crystalline object. It is just a little bigger than a pigeon's egg, set on a small golden crown. It is a mandarin button.

I first saw it more than 40 years ago, not in the sunlight but the moonlight, at three in the morning in September 1966 in the courtyard of our house in Beijing. Our head servant, whom I shall call Wang, pressed it into my father's hand. 'Keep this safe for me,' he said. 'It is the most precious thing I have. It belonged to my grandfather. The Red Guards are coming and I don't want them to find it.'

Sure enough, five minutes later the Red Guards burst into our house. One group went to the servants' quarters to ransack them, while my father stood in the centre of the courtyard in the moonlight with the mandarin button concealed in his hand. They came out five minutes later having found nothing and dragged Wang away for questioning. We never saw him again.

A mandarin button is a badge of rank. It sits on the top of a mandarin's conical hat, usually with a long feather attached. Mandarins are organised in nine ranks, from the highest, ruby, to the lowest, amber. Wang's grandfather was a third-grade mandarin in the court of the Qing emperor and therefore entitled to wear the sapphire button. If the Red Guards had found it, Wang would have been identified as a member of a once-privileged class and therefore deserving of special punishment. Sadly, despite many attempts, we have never been able to find out what happened to Wang nor to locate any of his remaining family to whom to return this precious heirloom.

The point of the story is that this totemic object was a powerful symbol in the world's first meritocratic bureaucracy. It was established in China in 605 AD during the Sui Dynasty. Unlike other court systems in which the retinue consisted of the nobility, in the mandarin system, mandarins were appointed through the Imperial examination system; a set of extremely rigorous written tests based on ancient, classical Confucian texts. Any adult male could take the exams and become a high-ranking official regardless of his wealth or social background. The mandarin bureaucracy was very successful and bound a quarter of the world's population into a single administrative system for one and a half millennia. It was finally abolished with the fall of the last Qing emperor in 1911.

In the middle of the nineteenth century, the British government was casting around for ideas on how to run their burgeoning empire. It commissioned a pair of Conservative peers, Stafford Northcote and Charles

Trevelyan, to come up with a paper suggesting how the administration should be organised. The resulting Northcote–Trevelyan report presented in 1853 became the founding document of the British civil service. Their proposal was, effectively, a direct copy of the Chinese Imperial system right down to the examinations on ancient texts, though in this case Latin and Greek rather than classical Chinese. To this day, top civil servants in Britain are known colloquially as 'mandarins'.

The essence of a bureaucratic system is a due process that is formal, logical and reasoned. Authority is not granted as a result of the brute force or even charisma of the leader. Authority comes from the role and not the person, from a set of hierarchical relationships and rules that govern who does what. The hierarchy tells you *what* you do, and the rules tell you *how* the job is done. The upside of a bureaucracy is that it is meritocratic; your level in the hierarchy depends upon your ability. The downside is that a bureaucracy removes judgement and choice from the work environment; bureaucrats are, in effect, just following the system.

As the world has become more closely interlinked and complex, bureaucracy has taken over. Bureaucracy is everywhere in the modern world because it is, technically speaking, the most efficient and rational form of organisation. But at its heart lies a crucial dichotomy concerning the concept of 'rationality'. The revolution in rational thought that drove the Enlightenment was based on using one's own reason rather than relying on the authority of others. To be a rational human was to apply the scientific method to challenging the status quo and working things out from first principles. But as soon as this scientific approach was applied not to the individual but to the organisation as a whole, 'individual' rationality was replaced by 'systemic' rationality in what is known as a catataxic shift. In a rational, bureaucratic system individuality is not a virtue but a vice. A bureaucracy removes judgement and choice from the individual because it is enmeshed one level higher in the design of the system.

A rational individual is trying to answer the question 'why?'. A bureaucracy is more concerned with the question 'how?'. To put it another way, individuals are concerned with the 'ends' but bureaucracies are concerned with the 'means'. In a bureaucracy, the 'means' becomes an end in itself.

The American sociologist Robert Merton provided a classic illustration of how, in a bureaucracy, following the rule becomes more important than the intention of the rule. Imagine a security guard checking passes at a factory gate in order to 'protect' the factory. The CEO arrives for a crucial meeting with the company's bankers, but he has forgotten his security pass so the guard refuses to let him in. As a result of the missed meeting, the bank forecloses on the company. The company is then bankrupt and the factory closes. The security guard thus causes the destruction of the factory by following rules designed to protect it.

Returning to the egg cup analogy, the bureaucratic focus on 'means' is represented by the walls of the egg cup. They are curved by design and lead ineluctably back to the point of maximum stasis: the bottom of the cup. The pea is gently steered back to its proper place in the gravitational hierarchy. No external action is required; it happens by design. But when a crisis occurs, the egg cup becomes inverted and the curvature of the walls compounds the problem by projecting the pea into the unknown. The bureaucracy becomes part of the problem. The conclusion we can draw is that, when a crisis happens, you should hire external consultants who can apply a different perspective, because your existing management bureaucracy is actually part of the problem. In a crisis, you need to focus on end goals more than means.

RULE 3. *When the crisis happens, bring in external consultants*

In the above discussion on bureaucracy, the analogies we used were very mechanical in nature. The notion is that a bureaucracy is a perfectible machine, like a precisely engineered Swiss watch. This is not true in practice, however, because a big gap exists between what the system is designed to be and what it actually is. Thus, not only do bureaucracies have an inherent problem with systemic rationality and a focus on means rather than ends, they also have a second problem. They are an imperfectible machine. The mechanical analogy is misplaced. This is a Swiss watch that can never be built.

The gap between policy and practice

A colleague was on a business trip to China in the early 1990s, travelling on internal flights using domestic airlines. As a health-conscious and wealthy Westerner, he would always insist on a seat in the no smoking section at the front of the plane. On this flight, to his great irritation, he found himself in a cramped seat in economy class, in the middle of a row of three. What was worse, he was surrounded on all sides (left, right, front and back) by Chinese passengers contentedly puffing away on their cigarettes. Petulantly, he summoned the air hostess to complain. 'This is completely unacceptable. I asked for a no smoking seat!' he barked. She replied, 'I'm so sorry, sir. Let me see if I can sort this out for you.' A few moments later, having consulted the passenger manifest, she came back all smiles. 'Don't worry, sir. It's all fine. I have checked and that seat you're sitting in ... that *is* the no smoking seat.'

As well as the pleasure derived from seeing a bullied minion win, the point of this story is that a big gap can be evident between the policies that an organisation has in place and the way in which they are implemented. The Chinese airline understood that some of its customers might be non-smokers. It duly had a policy for that. The problem was in the implementation of that policy: any seat that someone was not smoking in was a non-smoking seat, which, in effect, defeated its whole purpose.

If you were to ask a British company if it offered equal opportunities to men and women, it would probably answer in the affirmative. No doubt you would be shown a policy dealing with just that issue. In fact, despite any number of relevant policies, the ratio of women to men in senior management positions in the UK is 1:4.

Considering the number of compliance officers employed by banks before the Asian financial crash of 1997 might provide an even better example of the gap between policy and enactment. The compliance and legal departments of most major banks typically employed over a thousand staff. Despite the presence of all these compliance officers and the policies they produced, however, the crash and a string of subsequent scandals exposed alarming levels of malfeasance in the finance sector.

Every large organisation has a comprehensive set of policies covering issues such as worker safety, gender neutrality, environmental sensitivity and corporate entertainment. The provision of policies does not, however, guarantee compliance with them. Policies are often honoured more in the breach than the observance and it is often very easy to circumvent them.

The problem goes even deeper than this. Imagine an organisation in which every employee follows every single policy right down to the last letter. Would this situation represent perfection? The answer is no, as illustrated by the concept of 'work to rule'. When labour unions want to protest, they often impose a 'work to rule' regime in which workers follow their employment contracts to the letter, for example downing tools at precisely 5 p.m. every day. Operating in this way can cause major headaches for a company trying to respond to a rush order for an important client. A 'work to rule' regime can be one of the most effective weapons in a union's arsenal when attempting to bring management to the negotiating table.

If following the letter of the law can be disruptive, then clearly a gap must exist between what the rules say and what people actually do all day. The organisation expects employees to go beyond the letter of the law as defined in their contracts. So the dream of a perfect bureaucracy, with each employee a cog fulfilling its predetermined function and the whole meshing together into a perfectly engineered machine, will always remain just that – a dream. That Swiss watch can never be built.

Can corporate culture ever change?

Let's return to the issue of ignoring corporate policies. The 'work to rule' conundrum illustrates that there is something higher which is not captured by bureaucratic procedures and employee handbooks. This something is normally referred to as corporate culture. In order to change behaviour, it is culture that needs to change. Written policies only address the most pedestrian aspects of culture – the letter but not the spirit of the law. The usual way in which these higher level cultural aspects are addressed is through the creation of mission statements and core values and the example set by senior management. However, these methods may also be doomed to failure for a number of reasons.

Part of the problem is that the paradigm is still mechanical. The organisation is viewed as a machine and the manager is the engineer who will fix it. The only acknowledgement that we are dealing with people rather than cogs is a nod to biology in the form of a Darwinist metaphor, which usually runs along the lines of 'if you can't adapt to the environment, you'll become extinct'. It therefore follows that management must drive through the changes required by the increasingly competitive environment. To fail to change is to consign yourself to the scrapheap.

The first problem with this logic is that it is a misapplication of Darwin's theory. The point of his concept of natural selection is that it is the environment that does the selecting. That's why it is called 'natural' selection. If management does the selecting, it is artificial selection, much as a horse-breeder perfects a thoroughbred or a farmer gradually improves the quality of his livestock. So any manager who invokes Darwin has misunderstood the theory and should be viewed with the same scorn as the ghastly eugenicists of the 1930s.

The second problem is that trying to change corporate culture to align it with the changing environment assumes that the organisation is separate from its environment. In reality, the organisation is so intimately associated with its environment that it is not possible to separate it. Where would you draw the boundary line? It cannot be at the factory gates since this would ignore upstream suppliers and downstream customers. Likewise, if you choose to make the dividing line between those who are employed and those who are not, you exclude contractors, temporary staff, shareholders and a whole host of other stakeholders in the wider community. The organisation is part of its environment, not separate from it.

The answer to both of these problems comes with the recognition that culture is more of a bottom-up than a top-down phenomenon. It arises from granular activity at the lowest possible level; from the way in which people work together on a minute by minute basis. The best metaphor for corporate culture is not mechanical but biological: a murmuration of starlings on a summer's evening. As the birds flock together in the darkening sky, the patterns they make coalesce and then fragment in unexpected ways. This is emergent behaviour; a semblance of order arising spontaneously from below. The jittery and unstable conclave they make is half bounded and half free; halfway between being a coherent whole and a random collection of individuals.

This murmuration of starlings ties together most of the themes of this chapter. It is non-linear, unpredictable and full of unknowns. Each bird, every instant, is applying its own feedback control mechanism to avoid colliding with its neighbours. The flock as a whole will not succumb to bureaucratic control. It cannot be bounded by policies as it is not static. Any policy would be out of date as soon as it is written, like the generals studying the last war. You could take a snapshot of the flock and try to draw a boundary around it, but the next instant the shape of the flock would change and that boundary would no longer contain it. That does not stop those in charge from attempting to do it, though. It is the quixotic attempt to contain the flock through bureaucratic means that leads to one of the biggest issues for management, and particularly for crisis management: unintended consequences.

The eternal task of Sisyphus

A great deal of management time is taken up with correcting the unintended consequences of previous actions. However, the new actions will in themselves create unintended consequences. Since there is always a gap between the policy and the implementation, and the flock of starlings is never still, there will always be unintended consequences. So the job of management will never end – it is a Sisyphean task. What's more, it is often the case that managers move jobs before the consequences catch up with them so there is no one to blame, just a newcomer with a fresh, new policy to implement.

One of the more surprising aspects of quantum theory is the notion that the very act of measuring something changes its nature. This is famously illustrated by a thought experiment known as Schrödinger's Cat. It imagines a cat in a sealed box with a phial of poisonous gas, which will be released if a particular quantum event happens. It then poses the question, 'is the cat alive or dead?'. The answer, according to quantum theory, is that it is both alive *and* dead. It is the act of opening the box to find out that resolves the conundrum and forces the cat to be either one or the other. The act of observation thus changes the nature of the outcome.

A similar effect may be observed whenever an organisation introduces a new policy, such as a target to be achieved. Once a particular statistic is chosen as the yardstick with which to measure success, distortion is inevitably introduced. People begin to 'game' the system, changing behaviour to maximise that particular statistic often to the detriment of the overall goal.

Consider the following example. A company introduces a new client relationship management system. Sales staff are then informed that the number of calls they make to clients logged in the system will be measured. The volume of sales calls correspondingly increases, but revenues do not. Plenty of reasons may explain this outcome. Maybe fictitious calls are being logged. Maybe face-to-face meetings have declined because only phone calls count. Maybe sales staff are making lots of low-value, quick calls rather than having longer, more productive conversations. The system, after all, is recording volume not quality of calls. It doesn't really matter which explanation is correct, the point is that in attempting to measure you change behaviour.

In recent years, Western governments have adopted this 'management by measurable targets' approach. Examples abound of outcomes being almost the opposite of intentions. In the late 1990s the UK introduced school targets for GCSE grades. In an effort to improve standards, 25 per cent of pupils were expected to achieve grade C or above. As a result, teachers adopted a triage system, focusing on borderline candidates to the detriment of everyone else. Why waste time on the no-hopers? As a result, grades fell overall.

Another pertinent example is presented by the health care system. When the public complained that waiting lists in NHS hospitals were too long, the government introduced targets for waiting list times. No patient should have to wait longer than a certain time for a particular operation. Hospitals easily sidestepped this measure by creating an unofficial waiting list as a precursor to joining the official monitored waiting list. As a result, in many cases patients actually had to wait longer as they navigated their way through two waiting lists.

Setting targets thus creates unintended consequences. It also triggers a cycle of action and reaction. The unintended consequences created by target-setting are held up for public ridicule and a backlash against centralised control soon results. The mood of the public shifts and the populace calls for less bureaucracy and more freedom for hospitals to manage their own affairs. Freed from the stifling control of centralised target-setting, some hospitals thrive while others fail. Throughout the country, large differences in health care standards then emerge, which lead to a new scandal and accusations of the existence of a 'postcode lottery'. The obvious answer to this inegalitarian patchwork of privilege is to reintroduce centrally determined bureaucratic targets. We are back where we started and the whole cycle begins again.

RULE 4. *To prevent recurrence, change the culture as well as the policies*

To sum up, target-setting does not change the fundamental corporate culture but it does change the environment, usually in a way that 'games' the new targets and causes unintended consequences. The knee-jerk reaction to a crisis is to rush out a new policy backed by targets. This may briefly alter public perception but is likely to be ineffective in preventing similar crises in the future. Change has to come from the bottom up; from changes in behaviour, reinforced by peer pressure at the lowest level of the organisation and backed up by exemplary leadership at the top. Changing corporate culture is a long, slow process.

Time heals all wounds

The key feature of managing a corporate crisis effectively is the mastery of two contradictory impulses: speed and patience. These two traits do not sit comfortably together, but both are required in equal measure. As we argued previously, in order to control a crisis, the organisation needs to move faster than the speed of the story. So speed of response is clearly important. At the same time, patience is also important because change takes time, both of corporate culture internally and of public opinion externally.

The mood of the public is fickle, but this has one upside for those with a long-term view. No matter how bad a crisis, ultimately the public will change its mind and be back on your side, even if it takes decades. The public is easily bored and opinion leaders are constantly looking for views that challenge the status quo and can start new trends. The fashion industry hinges on this very fact. So it is part of the natural cycle of things that eventually champions are trashed and underdogs become popular. In a media-driven world, the archetypal stories for popular consumption are 'the mighty laid low' and 'the ugly duckling becomes swan'. Which one applies to you depends on where you are in the cycle.

Your crisis is being played out in a public arena and in the end it is the public who will absolve you. You cannot absolve yourself. Any protestations of innocence from the company at the heart of a scandal will be discounted as biased by the general public, who, on the whole, assume that where there's smoke, there's fire. If you want to change public opinion, you need a third party to speak up on your behalf; preferably an influential neutral organisation with an unimpeachable reputation or, even better, a personal endorsement from popular celebrity, which adds a believable human opinion to the debate.

RULE 5. *You can't clear your own name; only other people can do that for you*

Thus, while speed of response is required to manage the story, actively and vociferously protesting your innocence can be counterproductive. If someone denies something too much and too often, the public will assume they are lying. As Hamlet has it, 'the lady doth protest too much, methinks'. Patience is also required before third-party commentators, assessing the facts that have come to light, start to write sympathetic editorials about you. Even more patience is required before the legal system delivers its verdict, hopefully in your favour, and finally apportions blame.

Figure 3 lists the five key principles of crisis management. Our model is based on five themes – knowledge, public opinion, inertia, change and repair – and each theme has associated principles and rules. We refer to these themes as we examine the different case studies in the following chapters.

Theme	Key principle	Rule
1. Knowledge	Beware the unknown knowns. Someone in your organisation knows, but head office does not.	Rule 1: **Don't deny anything before you know all the facts**
2. Public opinion	A story develops a life of its own. To control it, you must move faster than the speed at which the story develops.	Rule 2: **Your response time must be faster than the speed of the story**
3. Inertia	Your senior managers will be trying to blame each other and preserve the status quo. They would prefer to manage the crisis inside the current organisational framework. Don't let them. You need independent, impartial advice from external experts.	Rule 3: **When the crisis hits, bring in external consultants**
4. Change	Every crisis has a silver lining: it's a catalyst for change. Learn from your mistakes and focus on changing the corporate culture, not just the written policies.	Rule 4: **Change the culture, not just the policies**
5. Repair	You can't clear your own name; only other people can do that. In time, if you have taken the proper steps, the public opinion will eventually change and become more positive.	Rule 5: **Be patient; recovery takes time**

Figure 3

So having spent a whole chapter setting out the theoretical considerations of crisis management, it is now time to start applying it in practice by looking at the issues of supply chain management in the next chapter.

CHAPTER 2

What's in my burger?

IT IS A COLD MORNING ON 28 JANUARY 1986. SO COLD IT'S CLOSE TO FREEZ-ing, which is unusual for Florida. A ring-shaped piece of rubber, as thick as your finger, is being pressed against two pieces of aluminium alloy. It is squeezed between the clevis and the tang of an aft field joint. It has been sitting there for months waiting for this moment. At 11.38 a.m., a mixture of aluminium and ammonium perchlorate in the adjacent chamber is ignited to deliver 150 million pascals of thrust. Under this enormous pressure, 1,500 times greater than the normal atmosphere, the gap between the clevis and the tang opens by half a millimetre. The rubber, made inflexible by the freezing weather, is unable to expand to seal this gap and a jet of flaming gas spurts out. It is clearly visible on the video cameras assembled to witness this event. Just over a minute later, travelling at twice the speed of sound and at twice the height of Mount Everest, the *Challenger* space shuttle explodes in full view of the world's press. All seven crew members are killed instantly, including Christa McAuliffe, a civilian who was to have been the first school-teacher in space. Schoolchildren around the world, gathered by their teachers around TV sets to watch a live broadcast of this inspirational moment, are slack-jawed and wide-eyed in shock and horror.

The explosion of the *Challenger* space shuttle, as with the 9/11 attacks on the World Trade Center, was a disaster that seared itself painfully into the national psyche; a moment captured live on television that no one watching would ever forget. So much else went up in flames at the same time: NASA's reputation, Ronald Reagan's space dreams, the engineering swagger of the US aerospace industry and the whole shuttle programme itself, which was grounded for the next three years. The commercial impact of this hiatus was that European Ariane space rockets became the preferred vehicle for launching satellites. This moment of hubris continued to resonate over the following decades and the *Challenger* disaster has been picked over by many commentators and analysts, each drawing a different conclusion from the tragedy.

The *Challenger* disaster is used as a case study on MBA courses to illustrate the dangers of groupthink. Political science students encounter it as a cautionary tale about political pressure overriding sound scientific advice. To engineering students, it is a cause célèbre that exemplifies the need to speak the truth to power. Statisticians use it to demonstrate the downside of assembling incomplete data sets when modelling risk. For sociologists, it is emblematic of the hazards of conformity to societal norms. PR gurus use it as an object lesson in how *not* to deal with a corporate crisis. As with all tragedies, the moral lessons are many and varied; however, bear in mind that they are only obvious with complete hindsight. The storm of opprobrium from opinionated onlookers must be balanced against the fact that 24 successful shuttle launches took place, using exactly the same methods and technologies, before the disaster struck.

We can draw out some common themes from the blizzard of criticism levelled at the *Challenger* disaster, without indulging in Schadenfreude or analytical smugness after the event. The best way to achieve this is to start with the facts and set out the frame of reference through which we will view them. This chapter is about supply chain risk. We will use the *Challenger* disaster as a case study on what went wrong between NASA and its suppliers and to consider the mistakes that NASA made in responding to the crisis. Then we will look at other illustrations of supply chain crises: Tesco's horsemeat scandal, Boeing's Dreamliner battery problem and Lehman Brothers' demise in the collateralised debt obligation (CDO)-driven banking crisis. In each case, the common theme is that a subcontractor further up the supply chain made errors for which the main contractor had to publicly assume responsibility. Each case offers lessons in how to deal with a crisis that was not of your own making but for which you will be held ultimately responsible.

Causes of the *Challenger* disaster

In 1973 James Fletcher, head of NASA, sold the space shuttle programme to Congress. Having successfully put a man on the moon, it was time to exploit America's leadership in space by broadening and commercialising their efforts. The Apollo programme had been all about prestige; pushing at the frontiers of technology regardless of cost. The space shuttle programme was offered as more of a business proposal. The 'one shot' Apollo rockets were hugely expensive but a reusable vehicle that could make a return trip to space many times offered substantial cost savings. Since the costs were amortised over the number of flights made, the savings depended on how many times a year the shuttle flew.

The name itself was marketing genius; a shuttle implies a regular commuter service, like daily flights from London to Edinburgh. In the plans put forward, the shuttle was intended to fly 60 times a year. In reality, it actually flew only six times a year on average. The turnaround time, which was supposed to take days, actually took months as a result of technical issues. For example, the 17,000 heat-insulating tiles that were glued to the surface of the spacecraft had to be individually inspected by technicians after each flight. With such low usage and such high maintenance and servicing costs, the cost per flight was more than ten times higher than planned. The mindset at NASA was therefore focused on fast turnaround times and as many flights as possible per year in order to make the shuttle a viable commercial proposition. Anyone or anything that delayed a launch was most unwelcome.

James Fletcher, who was overseeing the whole shuttle programme, was also on the executive committee of Pro-Utah Inc, a lobbying group that promoted investment in Fletcher's home state. Thus in 1973, when the contract for building the shuttle booster rockets was up for grabs, Fletcher steered it towards Morton-Thiokol of Brigham City, Utah. This was a surprising decision. Utah was so far away from Florida, and the booster rockets so large, that transport was a major problem. A decision was therefore made to make the rocket casings in smaller sections rather than a single unit. When these large metal hoops arrived in Florida they could be joined together and sealed with rubber O-rings. One root cause of the *Challenger* disaster is thus right there: engineering issues were rendered subservient to political machinations.

That was a decision taken more than a decade before the tragic accident. But the same theme was present in a decision taken on the evening right before the launch. On a teleconference on 27 January, the engineers at Morton-Thiokol expressed their concerns to NASA regarding the freezing temperatures at the launch site and the effect that would have on the rubber O-rings. Thiokol's technologists recommended a postponement of the launch, which the management of the Utah company also supported. NASA personnel, on the other end of the phone, were appalled and ridiculed their caution. They pointed out that there were two O-rings, so if one failed the other would be the back-up. Under pressure from NASA, Thiokol's management overrode the advice of their own engineers and reversed their decision. They called NASA later that evening to say that they had changed their minds and now supported a launch. Engineering concerns were once again quashed by a higher political imperative: NASA's desire to pack in as many flights as possible to justify the whole shuttle programme.

There was another political angle too. President Reagan, mindful of President Kennedy's PR coup, the space race of the 1960s, was keen to boost his own popularity with something similar. In 1984 he announced the 'Teacher in Space Project', whereby ordinary high-school teachers would travel on the shuttle in order to teach a 15-minute lesson from outer space. The aim of the project was to inspire students, honour teachers and spur interest in maths and science; all laudable goals whose PR benefits would rub off on the president. Christa McAuliffe from Concord, New Hampshire, was picked to be the first teacher to take part in this programme. Sadly, she would also be the last. When addressing the nation after the *Challenger* disaster, Reagan gamely tried to keep the programme alive. 'We'll continue our quest in space,' he said. 'There will be more shuttle flights and more shuttle crews and, yes, more volunteers, more civilians, more teachers in space. Nothing ends here; our hopes and our journeys continue.' Not surprisingly, the Teacher in Space project was dropped soon after. Having a teacher blown up on live TV in front of masses of children is probably the worst PR disaster imaginable.

The reaction

In the aftermath of the disaster NASA offered no immediate explanation regarding its cause, although it did suspend all shuttle flights indefinitely whilst an inquiry took place. The interim review board, appointed just hours after the incident, impounded all data and information regarding the flight. It took almost seven hours for NASA to confirm the deaths of the seven astronauts, all of whom, it claimed, died when the explosion occurred. NASA also discounted the theory that the cold weather at Cape Canaveral or an earlier accident several days prior to the launch had anything to do with the explosion. NASA's refusal to publish temperature readings, particularly when many were already suspicious that the flight should not have launched because of the cold, further damaged its public image.

Five days later NASA publically released footage showing the abnormal plume of fire and smoke venting from the right solid-fuel booster rocket. News reports and statements released by NASA were only ever short and gave little new information. NASA was heavily criticised for its reaction, particularly in newspapers such as the *New York Times*, which claimed: 'Shock, confusion and a lapse of self-confidence seemed to lead the space agency to ignore its own contingency plans for giving the public all the known facts in the first hours and days after the explosion of the space shuttle.'[6] The lack of information led to suspicion and speculation, something NASA had been keen to avoid.

In response to the tragedy, President Reagan ordered an inquiry into the incident. The Rogers Commission, named after its chairman, William P. Rogers, was charged with identifying how the disaster had come about and recommending how to prevent such an event happening again. All flights were suspended pending the results of the commission. After several months, the Rogers Commission published its report, which identified the failure of the O-rings to seal as the primary cause of the destruction of the *Challenger* shuttle. The failure was attributed to faulty design that may have been compromised by a number of factors, including the low temperature on the day of the launch. The report also condemned NASA and Thiokol for not responding adequately to the risk posed by the potentially faulty O-ring joints, instead categorising the danger as an acceptable flight risk. Furthermore, it became evident that the Thiokol engineers had known about the flaw since 1977. Since this time the problem had not only failed to be reported upwards to NASA superiors, but also failed to prompt the grounding of launches while a suitable solution was found. This blatant disregard was thus directly responsible for the deaths in the *Challenger* disaster. The official report concluded that: 'failures in communication ... resulted in a decision to launch 51-L based on incomplete and sometimes misleading information, a conflict between engineering data and management judgments, and a NASA management structure that permitted internal flight safety problems to bypass key shuttle managers.'

One colourful episode involved the theoretical physicist, Richard Feynman, one of the commission's best-known members. During a televised hearing, Feynman became frustrated with NASA's stonewalling and looked for some way to demonstrate that the problem lay with the O-rings. He called for a glass of iced water, ostensibly to drink, and dunked in it a sample of O-ring. On removing the chilled rubber from the glass he then demonstrated how brittle it had become. A live science experiment by a famous physicist thus eloquently illustrated the source of the problem. Feynman was so critical of NASA's failings that he demanded they include his opinions on the shuttle disaster or take his name off the final report. These observations, which were eventually included, highlighted the vast difference in risk-of-failure estimations between NASA's management and the engineers. NASA claimed that the risk of catastrophic failure was as low as 1 in 100,000. To put that in perspective, if a shuttle was launched every single day for 300 years there would, on average, be only one accident. A poll of the engineering staff put the risk of failure as high as 1 in 50. Feynman concluded, 'for whatever purpose, be it for internal or external consumption, the management of NASA exaggerates the reliability of its product, to the point of fantasy ... reality must take precedence over public relations, for nature cannot be fooled.'

Feynman, as a physicist, was clearly on the side of the engineers and cast the event as a morality play wherein the voice of scientific truth was drowned out by politics, PR and management pig-headedness. Edward Tufte, in his book *Visual Explanations*, drew a different conclusion. He pinned the blame for the *Challenger* disaster on the poor presentation of data. The engineers' voices may not have been heard, but it was their own fault because they presented the information so badly. To illustrate his point, he drew attention to the diagram (Figure 4) that Thiokol used to demonstrate previous problems with the O-rings.

As you can see, this diagram is dense with data. It shows the booster rockets in pairs, in chronological launch order, together with different temperatures and types of damage suffered. It is difficult to draw any conclusions from this diagram. The eye is distracted by the repeated images of the rockets and the key link between temperature and O-ring damage is buried in the detail. The data is there, right before your eyes, but it is impossible to see it. Tufte then points out that, had the data been presented differently, in a simple scatter chart like the

History of O-Ring Damage in Field Joints (Cont)

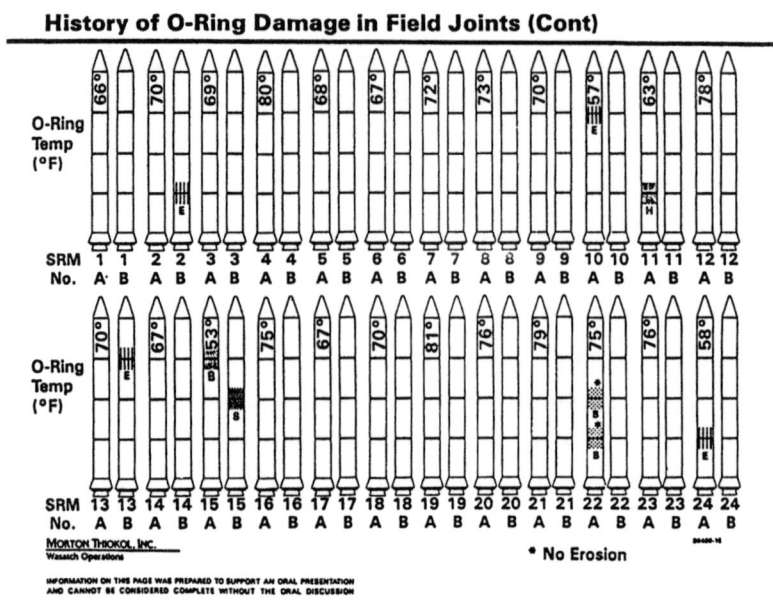

Figure 4

one shown in Figure 5, the conclusion that it was highly dangerous to go ahead with the launch would have been inescapable. It is clear just by looking at the chart that the temperatures on the morning of the launch were way below anything previously experienced. The graph also demonstrates a clear relationship between lower temperatures and O-ring damage. Tufte's point is that good graphic design can actually save lives.

The aftermath

On publication, the report of the Rogers Commission was greeted with a fair amount of criticism. Despite providing the names of some mid-level NASA employees, it did not identify any of those officials at headquarters who had pushed for the launch despite multiple warnings. In line with the commission's nine recommendations, NASA made a number of changes in both its administration and launch schedule to minimise risk and ensure another disaster did not occur. The O-ring

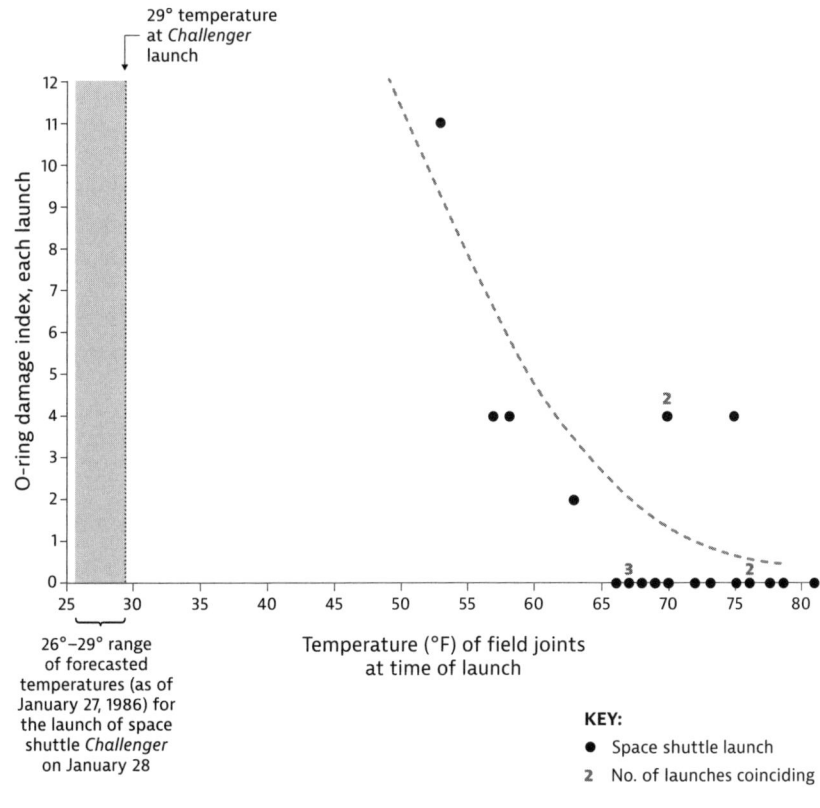

Figure 5

flaws were corrected in the redesigned booster rockets and a new Office of Safety, Reliability, and Quality Assurance was created within NASA.

Shelving its former highly optimistic launch schedule, NASA had a more realistic timeframe forced upon it. It worked alongside the Department of Defense to operate more expendable craft rather than shuttles. As a direct result, the shuttle programme was suspended for some 32 months before the next mission launched. The contract with Thiokol had included a $10 million penalty clause and the acceptance of legal liability in the event of errors causing 'loss of life or mission'. Thiokol in fact chose to accept the financial penalty in exchange for not accepting liability.

Although NASA made a number of changes to its systems in the wake of the incident, the management structure of the organisation and its working culture remained almost the same. In 2003 NASA's safety record was again questioned when the space shuttle *Columbia* disintegrated over Texas while re-entering the earth's atmosphere, causing the deaths of all seven crew members. Those who don't learn from their mistakes are condemned to repeat them. Indeed, the board investigating the incident stated that the lessons of the 'flawed decision making process' behind the *Challenger* disaster had not been learned, and thus had also led to the tragedy of the *Columbia*.

Lessons learned

If we refer back to Chapter 1 and the key principles of crisis management, we can see that NASA ignored almost all of them during this sorry episode.

Knowledge

The engineers at Morton-Thiokol knew about the severity of the O ring problem. They were unsuccessful in communicating this information, partly as a result of poor presentation and partly because NASA did not want to hear that message. This is a classic example of an 'unknown known'. Immediately after the accident, NASA's first response was to deny that the cold weather was a factor; however, it was later demonstrated to be the most important factor of all.

Public relations

NASA's communications with the press were terrible. Their instinctive reaction was to clam up and withhold information. This only made things worse, prompting speculation about a cover-up and a lot of negative commentary about NASA's management failings in the press. Though it is hard to put any positive spin on a disaster like this, an open, honest and communicative relationship with the press could have generated some sympathy instead of scorn.

Bureaucratic inertia
The huge gap between the level of risk estimated by management and engineers led to internal finger-pointing and apportioning of blame. It took external experts, in this case the externally appointed Rogers Commission, to address the issues and make recommendations on how the management structure at NASA should change.

Cultural change
Sadly, the recommendations of the Rogers Commission didn't really take root. Some superficial redrafting of policies occurred and some token supervisory appointments were made, but the culture and management structure didn't really change. This state of affairs was duly revealed in 2003.

The *Challenger* case is unusual in that the subcontractor actually warned the main contractor beforehand about the faulty part. Faulty parts and problems in the supply chain are usually only discovered after an accident has happened – and sometimes more than one accident. Now let's look at another case study, also taken from the aerospace industry, in which a supply chain issue was better handled. A clear link can be identified with the shuttle case study. Rockwell International, the main contractor for the shuttle, was bought by Boeing in 1996. Boeing's problems with the lithium batteries on its 787 Dreamliner are the focus of our next study.

The Dreamliner nightmare

In 1916 William E. Boeing founded the Pacific Aero Products Co. following the invention of his and Conrad Westervelt's B&W seaplane. The company was based in Seattle. This location was geographically remote but, for a company building wooden planes, access to a cheap and plentiful supply of spruce from the forests of Washington State offered a distinct advantage. By 1917 the company had changed its name to the

Boeing Airplane Company and worked on supplying the American Navy with seaplanes for the First World War. At the end of the war, demand for its planes collapsed, so Boeing diversified into furniture making, the supply of cheap wood again supplying a competitive advantage. In 1933 the company designed and created the first modern-day airliner, the Boeing 247, an all-metal, low-wing craft – safer, faster and easier to manoeuvre than other passenger airplanes. This plane was a spectacular success and Boeing soon became the dominant company in the commercial aircraft market, a position that it held for the rest of the century.

In the middle of the twentieth century, the main focus had been on building faster planes; a trend that topped out in the 1970s with Concorde, which proved to be uncommercial. The emphasis then switched to building bigger, long-range planes to satisfy the burgeoning demand for long-haul tourist flights; a market for which the Boeing 747, the world's first jumbo jet, was perfect. By the beginning of the twenty-first century, the demands of the marketplace had changed again. The 'hub and spoke' airline model was becoming outdated. Passengers no longer wanted to be herded like cattle between major international airports and then forced to catch another domestic flight to their eventual destination. Increased competition from low-cost airlines flying direct to small regional airports had introduced a new 'point-to-point' operating model that passengers preferred.

Reflecting this shift in the marketplace, when Boeing announced its latest, cutting-edge 787 Dreamliner aircraft in 2004 it was actually *smaller* than its predecessors, seating only 200 passengers rather than the 450 that could fit in a 747-8. The primary focus was operating efficiency. The smaller capacity fit the new point-to-point airline model and the use of advanced composite materials meant that fuel efficiency had been improved by 20 per cent. This was a significant advantage at a time of rising fuel costs and tightening standards for CO_2 emissions. The market responded enthusiastically to this new aircraft, gathering advance orders for 817 planes from 50 different customers – the strongest new-launch order book in Boeing's history.

A second different feature of the Dreamliner was in the way it was manufactured. The days when a plane could be built from timber from the surrounding woods were long gone. Boeing's customers were national airline companies all around the globe; countries who were keen to establish some sort of aerospace industry of their own. Boeing thus split the aircraft into a number of different sub-assemblies that could be manufactured by subcontractors in many different countries. If a local company had actually built part of the aircraft, a sale to the national flag carrier was more likely. Most governments view aerospace as a strategically important industry and decision-making involves factors that go beyond purely commercial reasoning.

As a result, the Dreamliner was the most international of all Boeing's planes. The wings were constructed in Japan (but the wing flaps in South Korea), the tail in Italy, the passenger doors in France, the access doors in Sweden, the landing gear in the UK and the floor beams (as well as some software) in India. All these sub-assemblies were delivered to Everett, Washington, to be bolted together into the final plane. In theory, this process would be far faster than normal, taking only three days on a lean and simple assembly line. An added advantage was that less inventory needed to be held by Boeing; much of it would be parked with the subcontractors at their expense.

So much for theory. In practice, assembling the Dreamliner was a nightmare. The maiden flight was originally scheduled for August 2007 but, as the deadline approached, Boeing announced a three-month delay due to production problems. A further seven production delays were announced over the next two years, much to the frustration of Boeing's customers. In the end, it was not until September 2011 that Japan's All Nippon Airways (ANA) took delivery of the first commercial Dreamliner to leave the production line. The reasons for the delays were numerous but all traced back to the fact that 65 per cent of the plane was built and designed by the global web of subcontractors. The first model to be assembled was 6 tonnes overweight, which meant many parts had to be redesigned in titanium. There was a critical shortage of fasteners; the nuts and bolts to hold the different subassemblies together. When the fasteners did arrive they often didn't work as intended or were incorrectly installed. Boeing ended up reworking many of the subassembly units because they simply did not fit together. The first three Dreamliners to come off the production line were unsellable because of these problems, causing the company to write off $2.5 billion.

The collective sigh of relief at Boeing when commercial deliveries started in 2011 was short-lived. At Boston Logan International Airport on 7 January 2013, an empty Japan Airlines Dreamliner caught fire after a battery overheated. Just two days later, on 9 January, a wiring problem was reported on a United Airlines Dreamliner near where the battery fire had occurred in the Japan Airlines craft. Two days after that the Federal Aviation Administration (FAA) announced a comprehensive safety investigation into the critical systems of the Dreamliner 787. Simultaneously, FAA head, Michael Huerta, sought to reassure the public that there was no reason to believe the remaining fleet of Dreamliners was unsafe.

But that wasn't the end. On 16 January 2013, the crew of a Dreamliner operated by ANA received a warning message about a malfunctioning battery and discovered smoke coming from some electrics – they made an emergency landing at Takamatsu Airport, and the passengers were evacuated on inflatable slides. As a direct consequence of the fire, all 787 Dreamliner series planes owned by ANA and Japan Airlines were grounded. Between the two airlines, this accounted for 24 of the 50 Dreamliners in existence.

That same day an emergency airworthiness directive from the FAA grounded all 787 Dreamliners operated by airlines based on American soil, until the problems relating to the lithium-ion batteries and the electrical system could be resolved. The directive stated that this measure was being taken because 'we evaluated all the relevant information and determined the unsafe condition described previously is likely to exist or develop in other products of the same design'. This was a serious step.

It was the first time in more than 30 years that the FAA had grounded an entire fleet; the same measure had been taken with the DC-10 in 1979. The Chilean, European and Indian equivalents of the US FAA also advised LAN Airlines, LOT Polish Airlines and Air India to ground their Dreamliners, and the Japanese Transport Ministry made the earlier groundings official. Other Dreamliner operators, Qatar Airways and Ethiopian Air, also made the decision to ground their planes until the issue had been resolved.

Boeing's response

On learning of the battery fire in Boston on 7 January, James McNerney, the CEO, requested information from the directors of the Dreamliner programme. Tom Downey, Senior Vice President of Communications at Boeing, stated: 'He want[ed] to know in real time everything that [was] going on.'[7] To some extent, the production problems that had plagued the Dreamliner for the last five years turned out to have a silver lining. The production manager in charge of the 787 Dreamliner programme had been replaced four times since McNerney took over the company in 2005. This revolving door in a critical position meant that the CEO had been heavily involved in investigations into the craft, and was therefore very familiar with all the issues related to the Dreamliner. In addition, Jim McNerney was an old pro, having cut his teeth at McKinsey and GE and spent five years previously as the CEO of 3M.

After suffering five incidents in as many days, the biggest challenge for McNerney was working alongside government investigations into the faults while also acting to resolve quickly the problem with the 787 Dreamliner before the plane's reputation was damaged. Immediately following the FAA emergency airworthiness directive, McNerney released a statement declaring that 'Boeing is committed to supporting the FAA and finding the answers as quickly as possible. The company is working around the clock with its customers, the various regulatory and investigative authorities.' On 18 January, Boeing made a further statement with regard to the 787s, announcing that all deliveries of new aircraft would be delayed until the battery issue had been totally resolved. Boeing worked alongside the FAA in the resolution of the battery issue, meaning that test flights to gather further information were permitted in early February.

Lithium-ion batteries are common in portable consumer electronic products such as laptops but were a new, untested technology in an aerospace setting. Their main advantage is that they are much lighter than their lead-based counterparts and store much more charge. Their disadvantage is that they contain a flammable electrolyte that must be kept under pressure – a problem on a jet plane in the stratosphere. The contract for supplying the lithium-ion batteries for the Dreamliner was originally signed in 2005 when the $LiCoO2$ batteries were the only type of lithium aerospace battery available. Since then, newer and safer types have been developed, which are more suitable for use on planes. The batteries, made by Rose Electronics, gained FAA approval in 2007, although with a list of nine conditionalities attached. Rather than using these batteries, those installed into the Dreamliner 787 were instead made by Yuasa. Following the grounding, Boeing worked fast to redesign the unit, improving the insulation for the eight cells in each battery, adding a stainless steel box to encase them better and adding a vent to direct any possible smoke or hazardous gasses out of the plane.

On 19 April, nearly four months after the FAA's emergency grounding, the US authorities gave Boeing the go-ahead to implement extensive changes to the plane's battery system. The FAA published details of alterations that must be made the following week, allowing Boeing and carriers to proceed with the necessary changes. Within a few weeks all batteries on the 50 Dreamliners in service had been replaced. In a CNBC interview on 17 June, James McNerney announced a high level of confidence in the resolution of the Dreamliner battery problem, stating: 'We have a very robust fix and a next-battery-generation system that I think is going to serve this airplane well for the future.'

Embarrassing, but not fatal

As the first fleet grounding by the FAA since 1979, the problems with the 787 Dreamliner were a major embarrassment for Boeing. They were also expensive; the four-month grounding was estimated to cost Boeing around $600 million. The two most affected carriers were Japan Airlines and ANA. The latter lost around $15 million as a result of the January disruption alone. Several airlines, including ANA and Air India, have since also voiced the need for direct compensation from Boeing, which they would prefer in cash as opposed to reductions in price on future purchases.

Boeing's reputation in terms of customers was also tarnished. As Charles Elson, Director of the John L. Weinberg Center for Corporate Governance at the University of Delaware, explains, 'It's never good for a company when you question its basic product, so now McNerney has to convince customers and investors that the Dreamliner is OK. This is a leadership test for him.' McNerney was perhaps fortunate in that, although the planes' substantial waiting list could have been damaged by these issues, the Dreamliner's main competitor, the Airbus 350, was also suffering development problems and was therefore unable to take advantage of the situation. Airbus could, however, learn from Boeing's mistakes. CEO of Airbus, Fabrice Brégier, released a statement regarding Boeing's problems on 17 January stating that his company was taking 'a lower risk approach' and using a 'more traditional' electrical system.

In all, Boeing's CEO Jim McNerney acquitted himself quite well. He took control of the crisis with decisive action from the start, avoided denials before establishing the facts, kept the press up to date with effective press releases and worked hard with all stakeholders, governments and customers to fix the problem as soon as possible. The damage to Boeing's reputation was temporary. At the end of 2013 it had 114 Dreamliners in service, with a further 1,030 on order, outstripping the order book of its major rival, the Airbus 350, by 25 per cent.

One of the most impressive statistics for the airline industry as a whole is its astonishingly good safety record. The best measure of transport safety is the ratio of number of deaths per billion kilometres travelled. For air travel, this figure is 0.05; for driving a car, it is 3.1. In other words, air travel is more than 60 times safer than car travel. Interestingly, the deaths per billion kilometres figure for the space shuttle is 16.2, which is still safer than walking (54.2), while riding a motorbike is practically a form of assisted suicide (108.9).

The explanation for the exceptional safety record for air travel can be traced back to the 1920s. A string of fatal commercial aircraft crashes in that decade meant the nascent industry had to dramatically improve safety in order to persuade passengers to fly at all. The Air Commerce Act was introduced in America in 1926, which established a raft of safety rules, pilot qualifications, aircraft inspections and carrier licensing. The concept of a pre-flight checklist led to a dramatic improvement in safety and has since been copied in other high-risk areas such as hospitals and construction sites. But the most important innovation was the certification by the FAA of the aircraft parts industry. Every part of a jumbo jet, down to the smallest bolt or fastening, is traceable back to its original supplier and is 'life limited'. In other words, each specific part has a recommended lifespan based on an estimated failure rate. After a set number of flights, that part must be replaced, well before it actually fails mechanically. This extraordinary level of traceability means that, when a problem arises, the faulty part can be easily pinpointed and remedial action swiftly taken, as with the Boeing Dreamliner case.

Ready meals: full of salt and Shergar?

Traceability is becoming increasingly important in another industry: food. The impetus for this development in Europe has, unfortunately, been more of a marketing exercise than a response to a safety issue. Under threat from cheaper agricultural producers around the world, the French began introducing the concept of 'terroir'. This term refers to a set of special characteristics in a local area – such as soil, topography and microclimate – that express themselves in agricultural products and make any produce from that place unique. The terroir concept is well known in the wine industry, whereby the French *appellation contrôlée* (AOC) system means, for example, that only sparkling wine made in the Champagne region can be called 'champagne'. In the last few decades it has been extended to cover a wide range of agricultural produce, examples being Roquefort cheese, Parma ham, balsamic vinegar, Puy lentils, Arbroath smokies and even Melton Mowbray pork pies.

The difference can be seen most clearly in the way that wines from the New and Old Worlds are labelled. New World wines tend to be classified by grape variety, such as Pinot Noir or Chardonnay. Old World winemakers emphasise terroir first. French vintners do not think that they are making a 'Pinot Noir' wine in, say, Burgundy. Rather, they are making a unique 'Burgundy' that happens to be made of Pinot Noir. The wine is an expression of the terroir, which cannot be duplicated even if using identical grape varieties and slavishly replicated fermentation and maturation techniques. The Scotch whisky industry has copied this approach, marketing single malts under specific distillery brand names (Laphroaig, Talisker, Glenfiddich) in preference to the blended mega brands (Johnnie Walker, White Horse, Cutty Sark).

Restaurants have also jumped on the terroir bandwagon; drawing attention to the quality of their ingredients helps justify higher prices. In recent years, restaurant menus have become ever more elaborate in their descriptions stressing the use of fresh, local ingredients. So 'fish and chips' becomes 'Line caught Dungeness cod in Ramsgate Ale batter with hand cut Kerr's Pink chunky chips'. At the bottom of the menu, next to the details of the obligatory service charge, will be a line stating something like 'All our ingredients are fresh and sourced from local suppliers who are well known to us'.

Supermarkets have followed suit. In an effort to halt the 'race to the bottom' of cut-throat price competition, most of the UK's major high street supermarkets stress quality as well as price. Their relationship with farmers has changed, at least according to their own marketing material. Where previously they would ruthlessly squeeze or switch agricultural suppliers to extract the last penny of profit, the current message is collaboration; developing long-term relationships with selected farmers to ensure they get the best, freshest goods produced in accordance with their ethical guidelines.

Supermarkets have been stressing food provenance and ethical treatment of animals in their marketing materials for several years. These are 'hot button' topics to a UK populace that has been sickened by TV exposés of battery chicken farms, industrial pig farming in filthy concrete sheds, mad cow disease, salmonella in eggs and other assorted food scandals. 'Trust us' is the message sold to the public by the supermarkets. 'We know where all our produce comes from. We buy from farms where the cattle each have their own passport. We can even tell you what field the cow that became that juicy rump steak grazed in.'

Against this background, when the press announced in January 2013 that a significant proportion of a Tesco beefburger was actually horsemeat, all hell broke loose. The public was enraged and disgusted in equal measure. Elderly equestriennes had the conniptions and the junior members of Pony Clubs up and down the country burst into tears. All that careful messaging about food provenance and quality was seen to be just a well-spun confection of hypocrisy and cant.

The scandal actually began in Ireland. The Food Safety Authority of Ireland (FSAI) first started investigating beef products in November 2012. Conflicting reports exist regarding whether the agency conducted the investigations randomly or was actually tipped off. Whatever the case, the FSAI spent two months carefully testing products before making an announcement. It wanted to be sure, as the findings were clearly going to be commercially damaging.

Finally, the FSAI informed the Department of Health in the UK, the Department of Agriculture, Food and the Marine, and the UK Food Safety Authority of the final results on 14 January 2013. Of the 27 beefburger products tested, 37 per cent tested positive for horse

DNA and 85 per cent tested positive for pig DNA. In the 31 beef meal products tested, none tested positive for horse DNA but 21 products tested positive for pig DNA. The Liffey Meats, Silvercrest Foods (both in Ireland) and Dalepak Hambleton (in the UK) processing plants were identified as the source of the contaminated beef products. As a result, supermarkets stocking products from these companies were advised of the findings. Tesco, Dunnes Stores, Aldi, Lidl and Iceland promptly removed the offending items from their shelves and offered full refunds for customers who had products in their homes. Other supermarkets, including Waitrose, pulled frozen beef products off their shelves, as a preventative measure to ensure that no horsemeat was found in their supply chains. Two days later, on 16 January, the horsemeat scandal broke in the press; the majority of reports focused in particular on a beefburger sold as part of the Tesco Everyday Value range that was found to contain 29 per cent horsemeat.

Tesco, the UK's biggest retailer, with a 30 per cent market share, was quick to react. As with the other implicated supermarkets, it withdrew all affected products from its shelves immediately and offered a full refund to any customers who had the contaminated products at home. Tim Smith, Tesco Group Technical Director, spoke about the withdrawal:

> We immediately withdrew from sale all products from the supplier in question. We are working with the authorities in Ireland and the UK and with the supplier concerned, to urgently understand how this has happened and how to ensure it does not happen again. The safety and quality of our food is of the highest importance to Tesco. We will not tolerate any compromise in the quality of the food we sell.[8]

Tesco quickly followed up on its initial response with a full-page ad released on 17 January in a number of UK newspapers, including *The Times, Daily Telegraph, Independent, Guardian, Daily Mail, Sun,*

Daily Mirror and *Daily Express*. The ad repeated the message that the offending products had been removed immediately and all affected customers would be refunded; in addition, it also made a promise: 'We will find out exactly what happened, and, when we do, we'll come back and tell you.' The fast response time meant that just a day after the scandal broke in the news, Tesco issued a lengthy apology and promised to keep the public informed of further developments. CEO Philip Clarke did not make the common mistake of denial (remember Rule 1); instead, he ensured that the issue would be looked into further and stressed that Tesco management was also shocked by the failure in its supply chain. A statement was also released apologising to customers further:

> We will not tolerate any compromise in the quality of the food we sell. The presence of illegal meat in our products is extremely serious. Our customers have the right to expect that food they buy is produced to the highest standards ... we apologise sincerely for any distress.

The company also launched an internal investigation into the source of the meat, as a result of which one of its suppliers, Silvercrest, was dropped because the 'breach of trust [was] simply too great'. In the relevant statement Tim Smith explained,

> The evidence tells us that our frozen burger supplier, Silvercrest, used meat in our products that did not come from the list of approved suppliers we gave them. Nor was the meat from the UK or Ireland, despite our instruction that only beef from the UK and Ireland should be used in our frozen beef burgers. Consequently we have decided not to take products from that supplier in future.[9]

On 6 February, Tesco and Aldi removed from their shelves Findus UK branded frozen beef meal products made by Comigel, stating that they did not conform to specifications. Tesco also removed its own Tesco Everyday Value lasagne 'as a precautionary measure' given that it was produced at the same site. Just a day later, the press reported that Findus 'beef' lasagne ready meals were made with up to 100 per cent horsemeat. Out of the 18 meals tested, 11 were found to contain 60–100 per cent horsemeat.

On 8 February, Prime Minister David Cameron condemned the scandal and called for further investigation into why 'when they thought they were buying beefburgers, they were buying something that had horsemeat in it'. He also referred to the horsemeat scandal on his press office Twitter account, stating 'this is completely unacceptable – this isn't about food safety but about proper food labelling [and] confidence in retailers'. This damning response further damaged Tesco's public relations efforts by calling into question the quality of the products sold at its stores.

On 14 February, a senior member of staff at Number 10 accused supermarkets of not doing enough: 'It is not acceptable for retailers to remain silent while their customers have been misled. The supermarkets need to justify their action and reassure the public.' The source also deliberately mentioned the lack of CEO engagement with the issue: 'The senior executives really need to explain how this has been allowed to happen. Some of these stores are responsible for a sizeable proportion of money spent on the high street and silence is not acceptable.'[10]

By 11 February, Tesco, along with Aldi and Findus, publically dropped Comigel as a supplier and issued an apology regarding the contaminated beef products. Tim Smith was again responsible for issuing a statement; he claimed that '[t]he level of contamination suggests that Comigel was not following the appropriate production process for our Tesco product and we will not take food from their facility again'.

In a direct response to Number 10's criticism, chief executives from Tesco, together with ten of the UK's largest food suppliers, published an open letter on 15 February assuring the public that '[w]e are openly sharing the results of these tests and acting immediately to withdraw any product where there is any doubt as to its authenticity' and '[n]othing is more important to us than our consumers' trust. We will do whatever it takes to restore public confidence in the food they buy and eat.'

CEO Philip Clarke chose to end his media silence by appearing in a video blog via Tesco's website. Clarke emphasised the importance of Tesco customers and stated: 'Nothing is more important to Tesco than the trust our customers place in us. And that trust depends on the quality of the products we sell.' In the three-minute video, Clarke described the new measures Tesco would be putting in place in response to the horsemeat findings, including a new benchmark system and direct and open transparency via the Tesco website regarding details of its supply chain.

Tesco ran a subsequent ad entitled 'What Burgers Have Taught Us' in February/March, in which it suggested that problems existed across the entire meat standards industry. The ad stated that: 'The problem we've had with some of our meat lately is about more than burgers and Bolognese. It's about some of the ways we get meat to your dinner table. It's about the whole food industry.' The ad was brought to the attention of the Advertising Standards Authority (ASA) after complaints that it implicated the whole food industry and not just the supermarkets that had fallen foul of the horsemeat scandal. The ad was subsequently banned. In response to the ASA ruling, Tesco maintained that it had not operated in a vacuum and that the problem was due to systematic failings in the supply chain. It claimed that the ad 'was to set out the action we had taken in relation to the horsemeat crisis and to acknowledge the fact the issue had serious consequences not just for Tesco, but for the whole of the food industry'.

Within a day of the story breaking, Tesco shares on the FTSE 100 fell by 1.1 per cent, losing around £300 million in market value as a direct result. Further, in the first financial quarter of 2013, Tesco sales fell by 5.5 per cent across Europe. Although the company reported a poor performance in electronics sales as the main factor, Clarke admitted that there had been a 'small but discernible impact' as a result of 'customer response to equine DNA being detected'. The scandal, although mostly an issue of food safety, revealed a breakdown in the supply chain, particularly concerning traceability. For competitors Morrisons and Sainsbury's, the scandal was used to highlight supply chain transparency. As Matt Piner, research director at retail consultancy Conlumino explains: 'Sainsbury's and Morrisons were able to spin the episode into a positive, highlighting their product quality ... for Tesco it merely raised some awkward questions and damaged shopper perceptions of the Tesco brand.'

The trillion-dollar burger

It should be no surprise that the product at the centre of the scandal was a beefburger – a beefburger is a supply chain manager's worst nightmare. It's fairly easy to establish the provenance of individual cuts of meat such as steak as they come from a single animal. But a beefburger is an amalgam of minced-up bits of beef, so unless you make the butcher mince a single piece of meat in front of you, you really have no idea where it comes from. Beefburger patties are made in industrial processing plants where the meat from many different animal carcases is mixed together. Economies of scale mean that batch sizes are becoming progressively larger. Often, fresh meat is mixed with frozen meat left over from an earlier batch. As a result, tests show that, on average, a beefburger patty contains meat from 55 different cows. And this figure can go as high as 1,000 different animals in the cheapest burgers made from the slurry from the slaughterhouse floor. At that sort of scale, the idea of tracing a single patty back to its 1,000 forbears is beyond practical reality.

As the commercial food industry gets bigger in scale, more global and involves more participants in the supply chain, provenance is an increasingly difficult thing to establish. For those who care about food, it's probably best to stick to small artisanal suppliers and to pay premium prices for the privilege. Everyone else needs to recognise that buying burgers is a leap of faith. You must pick a supermarket that you trust and hope for the best.

The 'what's in my burger' problem is wider than the food industry alone. The horsemeat scandal pales into insignificance alongside another example of the genre. This crisis almost brought down the whole edifice of global capitalism. The 'burger' in this case was a financial product known as a collateralised debt obligation (CDO) and the industry was the banking sector.

Though the worlds of food and banking may appear to be poles apart, a CDO is conceptually exactly like a burger. Instead of meat being minced up and repackaged, a CDO is an amalgam of debts; a set of cash flows from mortgages that have been split into tranches and repackaged. High-quality debt and low-quality debt is mixed together to ultimately create a product whereby risk is diversified as a result of this pooling process. A beefburger may contain some fillet steak and some less savoury elements like lips, eyelids and udders, but the end result is a bland, homogenised product of acceptable quality. Likewise, a CDO blends high-quality debt where repayment is almost guaranteed with risky low-quality loans where a default is very likely to make a product that is just good enough to qualify for institutional investment. As with burgers, where fresh meat is often mixed with an older frozen batch, some CDOs went on to be further blended with other CDOs to make a product known as 'CDO squared' (CDO^2).

The market for securitised mortgages like CDOs started in the 1990s and by 2006 had topped $2 trillion a year. This torrent of money had driven a boom in sub-prime mortgage lending; that is, loans to the impoverished to buy houses they could not afford and that were unlikely to be repaid. No one was overly concerned since house prices were rising fast and, at the time, it seemed like a one-way bet. When US house prices peaked at the end of 2006, the bubble finally burst. That's when the 'what's in my burger' problem became an existential crisis for almost every financial institution in the world.

The leap of faith you make when you buy a burger from a supermarket is known in financial circles as counterparty risk. This is sometimes more colourfully described by the aphorism 'it's only when the tide goes out that you discover who's been swimming naked'. Financial institutions, whose balance sheets held billions of dollars' worth of CDOs, found that they were unable to work out what it was that they actually held. The securitised mortgages had been so thoroughly blended it was impossible to estimate what the financial risks actually were now that the housing market was falling. The whole system was based on trust that the counterparty that issued the securities would honour them; but what if it declared bankruptcy? Someone would have to deconstruct each 1,000-cow burger to its original components and then estimate the health of each cow. There was a dawning realisation that this diversification strategy had not reduced risk but actually increased it. What if one sick cow had poisoned the whole batch? Everything was so convoluted and mixed up that no one knew what on earth was going on. The result was the worst financial panic since the Great Crash of 1929.

At the centre of this crisis stood Lehman Brothers. It had been an active participant in the CDO market and had a balance sheet stuffed full of securitised mortgages of dubious value. On 10 September 2008, Dick Fuld, CEO of Lehman Brothers, reassured investors during a conference call that things were fine. 'No new capital was needed,' he said, and then went on to state that the company's 'real estate and investments were properly valued'. It very soon became clear that this was not true. Five days later, the company declared bankruptcy. All the world could now see that Lehman Brothers had been swimming naked.

Bankruptcy occurs when a company's liabilities are greater than the assets on its balance sheet, meaning that the company is worthless. Scrutinising the balance sheet is one of the key criteria for evaluating counterparty risk. It tells you if the institution is financially big and strong enough to honour its debts. Lehman had been playing games with its balance sheet for some time using a mechanism called Repo 105.

A balance sheet is a snapshot of assets taken on a particular date. Repo 105 was a way of shifting debt off the balance sheet just before that date and returning it a few days later after the snapshot had been taken. Using this method, Lehman was able to shed $39 billion worth of debt from its balance sheet in the fourth quarter of 2007; this figure rose to $50 billion by the second quarter of 2008. By hiding the bad stuff for a few days each quarter when the inspectors came round to check, the bank could make its financial position look much stronger than it really was.

This wasn't the only way in which Lehman was misleading investors. In May 2008 Lehman reported a net worth of $26 billion. In September that year the bankruptcy administrator valued the company at minus $130 billion. In the space of four months Lehman had lost over $150 billion in value from its balance sheet. Some of this loss was due to the costs of unwinding trading positions in a falling market, but the administrator estimated these disorderly wind-up costs at just $75 billion. The conclusion must be drawn that the other half of the loss was due to the revaluation of overstated assets. In other words, the asset side of the balance sheet was carrying a lot of holdings at inflated values. So both the asset and the liability side of the balance sheet were bogus.

Most of this overvaluation of assets was the result of the 'what's in my burger' problem. The bank examiner's report (equivalent to a coroner's report on Lehman's corpse) was presented in March 2010 and illuminated the fundamental difficulties. Volume 2 of the report spent 500 pages focusing on the problem of valuation. It demonstrated that a full 18 months after the collapse of Lehman it was still impossible to properly work out what the CDOs on the balance sheet were actually worth; nobody could unravel them – not the bank examiner, not the accountants at Ernst & Young, not Lehman's own internal experts and certainly not the regulator.

Responsibility for valuing CDOs at Lehman was ascribed to the members of the Product Control Group; however, the amount of 'control' they actually had was nugatory. They rarely referenced external third-party prices when valuing securities and mainly relied on the trader's own in-house models instead. As page 547 of the report states:

> While the function of the Product Control Group was to serve as a check on the desk marks set by Lehman's traders, the CDO product controllers were hampered in two respects. First, the Product Control Group did not appear to have sufficient resources to price test Lehman's CDO positions comprehensively. Second, while the CDO product controllers were able to effectively verify the prices of many positions using trade data and third-party prices, they did not have the same level of quantitative sophistication as many of the desk personnel who developed models to price CDOs.

In other words, the people in charge of quality control weren't smart enough to understand the products they were supposedly supervising.

The collapse of Lehman Brothers was the biggest bankruptcy in US history and much of the blame can be laid at CEO Dick Fuld's door. Fuld, nicknamed the 'Gorilla' as a result of his pugnacious and aggressive manner, was voted the worst CEO of all time by Condé Nast in May 2009. He remains belligerent and unrepentant about the way he handled the crisis. In the Congressional Committee hearing on the collapse of Lehman in October 2008, Fuld still seemed to be in a state of denial regarding his role in the company's demise. It wasn't the reckless gambling by traders, balance-sheet shenanigans or lack of internal controls on his watch that were to blame; rather, the collapse was everybody else's fault. He explained the bankruptcy thus:

> Naked short sellers targeted financial institutions and spread rumours and false information. The impact of this market manipulation became self-fulfilling as short sellers drove down the stock prices of financial firms. The ratings agencies

lowered their ratings because lower stock prices made it harder to raise capital and [it] reduced financial flexibility. The downgrades in turn caused lenders and counterparties to reduce credit lines and then demand more collateral which increased liquidity pressures. At Lehman Bros the crisis in confidence that permeated the markets led to an extraordinary run on the bank. In the end despite all of our efforts we were overwhelmed.

Fuld, ever the narcissist, saw himself as the heroic captain battling against insurmountable odds. Henry Waxman, a Democratic Congressman from California on the Committee, saw things differently. 'Your company is now bankrupt and our country is in a state of crisis,' said Waxman 'You get to keep $480m. I have a very basic question – is that fair?'[11] You won't be surprised to learn that Fuld did indeed think it was perfectly fair. No one else did. Fuld joined Legend Securities in 2010 in an attempt to restart his career but was forced to resign a year later because he couldn't find anyone who wanted to do business with him.

To some extent, the steps taken in dealing with a corporate crisis can be mapped on to the psychological model describing the five stages of grief: denial, anger, bargaining, depression and acceptance. NASA, Boeing and Tesco suffered various degrees of damage depending on the skills of their CEO, but they all managed to get through to the acceptance phase and are still in existence today. Dick Fuld never got past the first stage and Lehman Brothers is no more.

CHAPTER 3

Says who?
Extraterritorial legislation

> You f***ing Americans. Who are you to tell us, the rest of the world, that we're not going to deal with Iranians.

THAT WAS HOW THE GROUP EXECUTIVE DIRECTOR OF STANDARD Chartered Bank responded to the Head of Compliance in the New York branch when questioned about the bank's dealings in Iran in 2006, according to the New York State Department of Financial Services (DFS). He got his answer soon enough, but it wasn't the answer he expected. In 2012, the bank paid a fine of $340 million to the DFS to resolve a dispute about its Iranian activities. Standard Chartered was also forced to appoint a monitor who would report directly to the DFS on the bank's internal procedures. In return, it was allowed to keep its New York banking licence.

It is perhaps natural to assume that the laws of a country apply only inside that country; however, in an increasingly globalised world, this is no longer the case. When a Hong Kong bank began to receive questions from New York about some transactions in Iran, it brushed them aside as being none of New York's business; the bank had been operating in difficult territories and emerging markets for 150 years. It had funded the opium trade in China in the nineteenth century, issued banknotes in its own name in Hong Kong and successfully navigated the upheavals of the Mao era and come out the other side stronger than before. So these enquiries from New York at first seemed like a cloud on the horizon no bigger than a man's hand. However, that cloud soon turned into an expensive and embarrassing typhoon that exemplified the extraterritorial reach of regulators in the modern world. This chapter looks at the risks posed by extraterritorial legislation and highlights some of the lessons to be learned. But first let's return to Standard Chartered.

Financing the empire

At the end of the British Empire in 1969, the two pillars of colonial banking, the Standard Bank of British South Africa and the Chartered Bank of India, Australia and China, merged to form Standard Chartered Bank, which began operating in New York in 1976.

The Chartered Bank had been founded by Royal Charter in 1858 and opened in Bombay, Calcutta and Shanghai. It expanded to Hong Kong and Singapore a year later, financing the British Empire's movement of goods from East to West, including cotton, indigo, tea, rice, sugar, tobacco, hemp and silk. This bank became even more important to East–West trade following the opening of the Suez Canal in 1869 and the extension of the telegraph to China in 1871. In 1957 Chartered Bank bought the Eastern Bank, together with the Ionian Bank's Cyprus branches, and established a presence in the Gulf.

The second of the two banks, Standard Bank, was founded in the Cape Province of South Africa in 1862 by John Paterson, and started business in Port Elizabeth in the following year. In South Africa, Standard Bank was notable for having supported the Kimberley diamond fields from 1867 onwards. It later extended its network further north to the new town of Johannesburg when gold was discovered there in 1885. By 1953 the bank had expanded in Southern, Central and Eastern Africa and had 600 offices, before merging with the Bank of West Africa in 1965, which led to an expansion into Cameroon, Gambia, Ghana, Nigeria and Sierra Leone.

Despite a strong presence in emerging markets, with two-thirds of its $6.5 billion worth of profits deriving from Asia, Standard Chartered is headquartered in London and is regulated by the Financial Services Authority. Its Asian focus was a big advantage in the banking crash of 2008 as it had little exposure to the US sub-prime mortgage market from whence the problems originated. By 2010, following the financial crash and the surrounding banking scandals, Standard Chartered was seen by many as the most reliable bank listed in London at that time.

Sir John Peace, chairman of Standard Chartered, had a prestigious list of past achievements, including being chairman of Experian and Burberry and former boss of Great Universal Stores (GUS) and having had a distinguished career in the army. Peter Sands, CEO, and Richard Meddings, finance director, were also widely respected; in early 2012 both had been tipped for the role of governor of the Bank of England.

The Iranian sanctions

In 1997, President Bill Clinton issued Executive Order 13059, which decreed that 'virtually all trade and investment activities with Iran by US persons, wherever located, are prohibited'. The US had first initiated sanctions against Iran in 1979, when the Islamist uprising deposed the shah and militants in Tehran took 52 Americans hostage inside the US embassy. Since 1997 the sanctions had been further tightened; in 2010, for example, the importation of Iranian carpets to the US was prohibited. Violations of the Iranian Transactions Regulations – a criminal offence – can be penalised by a $1 million fine and/or a 20-year jail sentence. The Office of Foreign Assets Control (OFAC), part of the US Treasury Department, implements this legislation. It also regulates trade with other countries, such as North Korea.

Before 2008, 'U-turn transactions' were permissible under US law. This meant that an entity based outside the USA, such as a foreign institution, could transfer money through the USA to another institution that was also based outside the country. U-turn transactions thus allowed money to be moved for Iranian clients among non-Iranian foreign banks, such as those in Britain and the Middle East, and cleared through the US so long as the transactions neither started nor ended in Iran. These payments were closely monitored to ensure that no suspicious activity was taking place. US clearing banks monitored the wire-transfer messages they received from the other banks involved and, if they didn't have the necessary information, required them to freeze the assets.

In 2008, the USA tightened its approach to Iran as it suspected that the country was financing nuclear weapons and missile programmes using banks such as the Central Bank of Iran/Markazi, Bank Saderat and Bank Melli. U-turn transactions were banned entirely.

The New York regulator's complaint
In October 2011 the DFS was created; its remit was reforming the regulation of New York's financial services industry. It supervises 4,400 institutions, which comprise assets of around $6.2 trillion. In October 2004, Standard Chartered Bank had been ordered by New York State and the Federal Reserve Bank of New York to adopt acceptable Bank Secrecy Act/Anti-Money Laundering practices with respect to foreign bank correspondent accounts. The order also instructed it to employ an independent consultant to report to the regulators on the bank's conduct and to perform a retrospective 'look back' transaction review, for the period of July 2002 to October 2004.

Deloitte, one of the so-called 'Big Four' professional accountancy firms, was advising Standard Chartered. However, the results of a DFS investigation in August 2012 revealed that Deloitte had aided and abetted the bank's illegal activities by sharing confidential data about other clients' similar illegal activities and by watering down its reports to the regulators.

To avoid the scrutiny of the regulators, Standard Chartered Bank amended Deloitte's draft (and supposedly impartial) report, removing any mention of payments that would reveal their illegal activities. In an email recovered by the regulators, the global leader of Deloitte's Anti-Money Laundering/Trade Sanctions practice confessed: 'This is too much and too politically sensitive for both Standard Chartered Bank and Deloitte. That is why I drafted the watered-down version.'

The DFS was investigating other banks at the time, including HSBC, which also had a colonial heritage and strong foothold in Asia. In early 2012, HSBC was accused by the US Senate of failing to prevent money laundering by various countries around the world, including Mexico and Iran. Then, in July 2012, a Senate panel report claimed that HSBC was being used by Mexican drug cartels, Saudi Arabian banks with terrorist connections, and certain Iranians who were evading US sanctions. The report claimed that, between 2001 and 2007, 28,000 undisclosed sensitive transactions had been carried out by HSBC's American wing, as uncovered by an internal audit. Around $19.7 billion worth of these – a huge majority – involved Iran.

Furthermore, it was reported that HSBC Middle East and HSBC Europe had intentionally and repeatedly changed transactional data to make it look as though Iran was not involved. At this point it was not yet clear which of these cases had broken US law – if any. The Dutch bank ING was also targeted. A settlement of $619 million was reached in June between ING and the Justice Department/New York County district attorney's office. It was the largest fine ever imposed on a bank in response to US sanction violations – in this case for illegally moving billions of dollars on behalf of Iranian and Cuban bodies.

In relation to anti-money laundering regulations, the banks had a very simple strategy – they just ignored them. What a bank official later described in a Senate report as a 'lack of a compliance culture' delivered massive profits. In 2007 and 2008, HSBC Mexico wired $7 billion to US dollar accounts in New York; more money than even bigger Mexican banks wired to US accounts. A subsequent investigation by the US Senate Permanent Subcommittee on Investigations quoted an

HSBC email lamenting how the bank would lose $2.6 billion in revenue from US dollar accounts after the practice was stopped.

The bank's miscalculation was to underestimate the growing extra-territorial power of the US regulators. For Standard Chartered Bank, matters came to a head in August 2012 when the DFS filed a 27-page complaint against it. This document asserted that the bank had conducted itself in an intentionally fraudulent manner; first, in moving $250 billion (in over 60,000 transactions) for sanctioned Iranian clients through its New York office and, second, in attempting to cover up its actions. These clients included state-owned institutions such as the Central Bank of Iran, Bank Saderat and Bank Melli. The charge sheet, so to speak, read thusly, accusing it of:

- Falsifying business records
- Failing to maintain accurate books and records
- Failing to report misconduct to the regulator in a timely manner
- Evading Federal sanctions

It appeared that the New York branch had been used, in practice, 'as a front for prohibited dealings with Iran – dealings that indisputably helped sustain a global threat to peace and stability', according to the DFS. It also demanded that the bank attend a hearing, under threat of revoking its licence to trade in the city.

The most damning evidence included the existence of a code name (Project Gazelle) for surreptitious dealings as well as an in-house manual that explained how to automate the covering up of illicit dealings. Evidence also existed of money flowing to Iran's central bank and the US executives' dire warnings of 'criminal liability'. The bank was also accused of doctoring wire transfers by concealing the identities of Iranian clients. Incredibly, manuals summarising their illegal practices were even provided by executives, including one entitled 'Quality Operating Procedure Iranian Bank Processing'.

Emails revealed that the bank's legal team had been giving detailed advice on how to evade sanctions as far back as the mid 1990s. In one such email, from March 2001, a Standard Chartered lawyer advised that 'our payment instructions [for Iranian entities] should not identify the client or the purpose of the payment'. The DFS also alleged that Standard Chartered had 'similar schemes' in place for other countries under US sanctions, including Libya, Sudan and Myanmar (formerly Burma).

This behaviour over the course of nearly two decades had not passed without internal dissent. The bank's chief executive for the Americas wrote to his bosses in London in 2006, reporting that the transactions had 'the potential to cause very serious or even catastrophic reputational damage to the group'. He received the reply: 'You fucking Americans. Who are you to tell us, the rest of the world, that we're not going to deal with Iranians.' There was no way of knowing how much or how little of the money had been used by Iran in its nuclear programme or to fund terrorist organisations. The regulator demanded a meeting with the bank on 15 August.

With a business model based on circumventing regulation, when wrongdoing was publicly exposed, it did not come as a bolt out of the blue; the only surprise was that the bank had been caught, not that it had occurred in the first place. And the public exposure afforded by the world of 24-hour rolling news and the internet meant that reputational damage on top of regulators' fines was a new force the bank had to reckon with.

The reaction

On receiving the complaint from the DFS, Standard Chartered Bank issued a global press release on 6 August 2012, defending the results of its review, its disclosure to US agencies and its 'overwhelming' compliance with US sanctions and regulations. In a second statement, the bank said it 'strongly rejected the position or the portrayal of facts as set out'. The accusations had appeared shortly before the close of the London Stock Exchange and, despite Standard Chartered's rebuttals, the share price registered a record fall in the FTSE 100, dropping by 6 per cent to just under £15.

It seemed the bank was not prepared for the intensity of public reaction, despite having admitted in previous annual reports that it was in negotiations with the regulators in relation to broken sanctions.

Standard Chartered's chief executive, Peter Sands, cut short a holiday and flew home. Speaking to the *Daily Telegraph*, he implied that the DFS order was unnecessary and everything had been in hand: 'We were surprised to receive the order, given that discussions with the agencies were ongoing. Resolution of such matters normally proceeds through a co-ordinated approach by such agencies.' He added: 'We are working out our next steps and liaising with the other agencies in the US and, of course, the FSA.'

Some British politicians, as well as the *Daily Telegraph*, reacted by accusing the DFS of trying to undermine the London financial markets. London Mayor Boris Johnson urged that 'proper desire to root out wrongdoing' not turn into 'protectionism' and 'self-interested attack'.

Shock and anger were expressed by investors in response to the sharp fall in share price. Anger was directed not only at the bank's management but also at the DFS and its superintendent, Benjamin Lawsky, as a result of the manner in which the regulator had handled the issue. There were accusations of hounding, public shaming, personal glory sought by Lawsky himself and a sinister attempt by the American regulator to gain jurisdiction in foreign markets where it had no business.

Mindful of the damage that this unquantified regulatory risk was doing to the bank's share price and reputation, Standard Chartered was keen to resolve the issue as soon as possible. Seven days after the crisis first emerged, the DFS announced that a settlement had been reached which involved Standard Chartered paying a fine of $350 million. But this was by no means the end of the story. Other US regulators at a Federal level were incensed that the DFS had not kept them in the loop[12] and that Lawsky had conducted a lone crusade all the way to the settlement, leaving them in the dark. Both the Federal Reserve and OFAC at the US Treasury appeared to have been asleep at the wheel. Lawsky was only a state-level regulator.

To put this situation in context, let's reframe it in UK terms. Imagine if Kent County Council took a vote on denouncing Robert Mugabe's regime in Zimbabwe. A local councillor then spots a branch of, say, Citibank, in a local high street and successfully extracts a $350 million fine from it because Citibank's New York headquarters has conducted some transactions with a few customers in Zimbabwe in the past. The two obvious questions that would arise are: 'why would Citibank pay such a huge fine to such a low-level regulator?' and 'if Citibank has really done something wrong, why is the UK government not investigating it?'

If Standard Chartered hoped that this swift settlement would draw a line under the issue and allow it to move on, it was sorely mistaken. Both the Federal Reserve and OFAC announced that they would be conducting their own investigations into the affair. Shareholders also remained rather confused. Having issued a vehement denial in their press release on 6 August, why did the bank agree to a huge financial settlement only one week later? Either it had broken Rule 1 of crisis management and denied something in public before it had full possession of the facts, or it was knowingly lying. Either way, the bank didn't look good. According to the *Daily Telegraph*,[13] one shareholder said: 'What is not clear is why their position changed so radically. If they did not breach the rules, why have they agreed to pay the settlement and open themselves up to further fines with other US regulators?' Others inferred that the Singaporean government, which owned 18 per cent of Standard Chartered through its sovereign wealth fund Temasek, had forced the reluctant board to accept the settlement.

The Federal-level investigations were finally concluded five months later. In December 2012, Standard Chartered announced that it had reached an agreement with the Federal Reserve and OFAC involving a further fine of $327 million; fines now totalled $677 million. Even this, however, was not the end of the story. At a conference in March 2013, while talking publicly about the bank's financial performance with economics experts, Standard Chartered chairman, Sir John Peace, was asked a question about bonuses. If the bank had paid such colossal, record-breaking fines for illegal trading, why had top executives received huge bonuses? Proving that neither he nor the bank had got past Rule 1 and were still in the denial phase, he responded: 'We had no wilful act to avoid sanctions; you know, mistakes are made – clerical errors – and we talked about last year a number of transactions which clearly were clerical errors or mistakes that were made.'[14]

With the terms of the settlement including an admission of guilt, this statement did not go down well and the US authorities were swift to make their displeasure known. In an embarrassing climb-down, a week later, Peace was forced to issue a second statement accepting that the bank had, in fact, engaged in wilful criminal conduct:

> My statement that [Standard Chartered] 'had no wilful act to avoid sanctions' was wrong, and directly contradicts [Standard Chartered]'s acceptance of responsibility in the deferred prosecution agreement and accompanying factual statement. Standard Chartered Bank, together with me, Mr. Peter Sands and Mr. Richard Meddings, who jointly hosted the press conference, retract the comment I made as both legally and factually incorrect. To be clear, Standard Chartered Bank unequivocally acknowledges and accepts responsibility, on behalf of the Bank and its employees, for past knowing and wilful criminal conduct in violating US economic sanctions laws and regulations, and related New York criminal laws, as set out in the deferred prosecution agreement. I, Mr. Sands, Mr. Meddings, and Standard Chartered Bank apologize for the statements I made to the contrary.[15]

This statement has to be chalked up as a comprehensive win for the US regulators. The court of public opinion is still divided, however. Some still view a New York State regulator deciding which customers an Asian-based bank can deal with as a gross example of extraterritorial meddling. The USA may place Iran on its 'Axis of Evil' but does it have the moral right to bully everyone else into accepting their view? The alternative view is that a bank with a long history of dabbling in dangerous places had a lax compliance regime and was playing fast and loose with the rules. It got what it deserved. The view that you take probably depends on your nationality, but one conclusion is clear: extraterritorial regulatory enforcement poses a significant risk to multinational organisations and can end up being very expensive indeed.

Not only are these kinds of crisis financially and reputationally costly but after years of deregulation/self-regulation, the tide is turning toward more, and more rigorously enforced, regulations and increased efforts to see those at the top held accountable. Or as Robert Mazur, who infiltrated the Medellín cartel during the prosecution and collapse of BCCI, said, 'the only thing that will make the banks properly vigilant to what is happening is when they hear the rattle of handcuffs in the boardroom'.[16]

The public fallout and reputational damage suffered by Standard Chartered was considerable, and at every stage as the crisis unfolded, it contrived to make things worse. Instead of contrition, and a change of culture, it offered bluster and lazy rationale until eventually forced from denial into an embarrassing climb-down.

Extraterritorial jurisdiction means, literally, the power of a government to exercise authority beyond its boundaries. This legislation should come under 'known knowns'. Ignorance of the law, as any schoolchild will tell you, is no defence. And it should never come as a bolt out of the blue. Even Standard Chartered was warned internally that its actions had 'the potential to cause very serious or even catastrophic reputational damage to the group'– but chose to ignore those warnings. Implementing effective business forecasting, risk assessment and due diligence is not a legal nicety but a corporate financial and reputational necessity.

The problems are manifold. A boom in international trading, especially over the internet, and multinationals operating in multiple jurisdictions mean there is a constant need to keep up with ever-shifting legal frameworks. And just because something is fine in one place, for example 'lavish gift giving', does not make it exempt to regulations elsewhere. If a business is based in, or even just passes through, the UK or the US, the practice of gift giving will be subject to the laws in the UK and the US. An organisation must make sure that it breaks no laws, or, if it chooses to do otherwise, as did Standard Chartered, it must make an informed decision about doing so and be aware of the consequences.

Cases will always exist of crises occurring as a result of 'unknown knowns' – facts known at some lower level in the organisation but that the CEO is unaware of. However, to avoid the rattle of handcuffs, the chain of command must be clear and effective compliance procedures established and followed.

The rock of regulation and the whirlpool of public opinion (see Chapter 5) are two risk factors no company or CEO can afford to ignore. The rise in class action lawsuits, whereby aggrieved members of the public gather together into a large group to collectively sue a corporation, means the potential financial repercussions of corporate wrongdoing are increasing dramatically.

In short, now is not the time to underestimate the extraterritorial power of regulators. It is the new culture of our times.

The end of globalisation

Towards the end of the twentieth century, 'globalisation' was the word on every CEO's lips. But in recent times globalisation appears to be in reverse. The dream of a world without borders is receding as local concerns begin to reassert themselves. Take the recent experience of Berkshire Hathaway's bid to take over Heinz, the ketchup and beans company. Warren Buffett had to fly to China in order to smooth the path for the deal with the Anti-Monopoly Bureau in Beijing. You may wonder why Chinese officials should have a say in whether one US company buys another US company. The answer is that Heinz is a multinational with revenues in China and therefore is subject to Chinese anti-trust legislation. This is by no means an exceptional case. In a large takeover bid, a multinational may have to win approval from the regulators in as many as 100 countries before the transaction can be completed. In the mining sector, Xstrata announced its plan to buy Glencore at the beginning of 2012. Eighteen months later lawyers are still toiling away in a multitude of jurisdictions trying to gain clearance from the local regulators. For example, China has demanded that Xstrata sells its holdings in a Peruvian copper mine before passing the deal. The advantage to China is that doing so will weaken Xstrata's ability to control copper prices in the Chinese market.

Even in less-developed economies, local regulators are beginning to flex their muscles. African regulators now demand the right to review any deal involving a company with operations in two or more countries in the COMESA area (the East and Southern Africa Common Market). Multinationals, who up until now have been able to do pretty much whatever they liked in Africa, may now have to get a potential Zimbabwean deal cleared by an Ethiopian regulator.

The most potent symbol of a borderless future is the World Wide Web but even this is under attack. The internet is still growing in size but the web isn't. Back in 2000, these two terms were almost synonymous but today only a quarter of internet traffic flows through the web. The rest flows through private semi-closed platforms that use the internet for transporting data but don't use a web browser to display it. If you check your email on your mobile phone, post something on Facebook, have a Skype conversation, tweet on Twitter, play with some Apps on your iPad or watch a film on LoveFilm's streaming service you use the internet but not the web. At its launch, the web represented a utopian ideal of the whole world being brought together to share information in cyberspace using a single common language known as

HTML. But this borderless dream of communal space is rapidly being replaced by a series of walled and gated, members-only communities. This situation is the cyber equivalent of the enclosure of the commons in the sixteenth century.

In the finance sector, global flows of capital are waning as cross-border lending by banks has fallen sharply. The Bank for International Settlement (BIS) tracks how much banks lend to other banks overseas. In 2005 cross-border interbank loans represented 46 per cent of all lending. By 2012 this had fallen to a historic low of 38 per cent. The change has been driven by new regulations in the home market that require banks to hold more capital in reserve. To rebuild their damaged balance sheets, banks are pulling back money from overseas and focusing instead on their local markets. National governments, who have bailed out banks, would prefer to see that capital at work in their own territories.

The same trend can be seen in the widespread reintroduction of capital controls – dams that trap pools of financial liquidity inside a country. A study by the International Monetary Fund noted that, in 2000, some 20 capital control measures were introduced worldwide. In contrast, in 2012 120 controls were introduced – a sixfold increase. The overriding conclusion to be made is: global banking is out of fashion; local is the new vogue.

At a more prosaic level, many governments are looking to reduce their towering burdens of debt by increasing their tax take. This strategy is developing into a two-pronged attack, focusing on closing offshore tax havens and introducing new locally based taxes such as a 'mansion tax'. Both of these trends can be described as 'anti-global'. Offshore tax havens are reservoirs of global capital – money without borders. In closing them or introducing stricter disclosure rules, Western governments are forcing this cash back onshore. Also, any swing towards taxing property in preference to income is a move towards localism. It is hard to determine the geographic location from which income actually arises, a loophole well used by tax consultants. But there can be no argument about the location of a property and local authorities can make a very informed estimate of its value.

Looking to the future, we see a vision that is similar to the remote past. In medieval times, there was no unitary authority but rather a series of overlapping obligations and jurisdictions in a patchwork of non-exclusive arrangements. In England, there were three different jurisdictional structures: the parish, the manor and the hundred. So, for the same plot of land, you paid tithes to the Church, heriot to the manor and frankpledge to the hundred. What's worse, the borders of these three systems did not coincide and, as a result, different fields in your smallholding could also belong to different manors or parishes. Overall, it was a legislative mess that was not cleaned up until the nineteenth century when a unitary system of local government was introduced and the boundaries were harmonised.

As 'global' declines and 'local' gains in importance, we are returning to the legislative patchwork of medieval times. In a world of multinationals, regulators are no longer content to stay within their own borders but seek to apply their rules outside their national boundaries. A Chinese regulator can force a Swiss company to sell its stake in a Peruvian mine. A New York district attorney can fine Hong Kong's Standard Chartered bank for conducting business in Iran. Our conclusion here is that the legislative burden is increasing dramatically, driven by officious national regulators buoyed up by the new 'local' zeitgeist as globalisation is pushed into reverse.

Extraterritorial reach: the long arm of the law

To illustrate the reach of extraterritorial powers in the modern world, consider the hypothetical examples below. Which do you think are legally justified?

- Can the head of state of a country that tortures suspected terrorists be arrested and tried when he travels to another country where torture is illegal? For example, could President Obama be locked up in a Spanish jail for torturing Iraqi prisoners in Guantanamo Bay?

- If a court in Country A wants to put a citizen of country B on trial, can Country A demand that the suspect be handed over without providing a reason or supplying any sort of supporting evidence beforehand?

- A jury in Country G indicts a citizen of Country H believing it has probable cause. Does the foreign citizen need to be informed or can the indictment be 'sealed' so that the first time the foreign citizen discovers he is a suspect is when he is arrested at the airport? What if he is arrested in transit between two other countries and has not gone through immigration yet?

- A website in Country K is selling Nazi memorabilia. Doing so is illegal in Country J. The two countries speak different languages; thus, for Country J's consumers, the website is in a foreign language. Can Country J prosecute the company behind the foreign website even though it is unintelligible to its citizens?

- Two companies in Country P collude to fix prices. Doing so is perfectly legal in Country P but illegal in Country Q. The companies in question also sell some products in Country Q. Can a court in Country Q prosecute the companies even though the price fixing is happening in a different country?

- A Chinese company pays a bribe to win a contract in Africa. The Chinese company has a secondary listing on the New York stock exchange. Can the Chinese company be prosecuted for corruption under US law when its only connection with the United States is that listing?

- An Egyptian company employs an agent in Kazakhstan who uses bribes to influence local officials. The Egyptian company also has a small subsidiary in the UK. Can a director of the UK subsidiary be prosecuted even though his company has nothing to do with Kazakhstan?

The answer to all of the above questions is 'yes', which shows that extraterritoriality has far wider implications than you may at first suppose.

Of course, claiming extraterritorial jurisdiction is one thing. Exercising it is another. For the claim to be effective without the use of force, it must be agreed upon by the authority in the external territory. One problem with enforcing universal jurisdiction is the need for the subject to be present in the state exercising that jurisdiction. If the accused, as is likely, fails to voluntarily attend, the state relies on extradition, normally exercised through bilateral treaties. Such treaties used to require the offence be a crime in both states but recently this principle has been subject to erosion. The extradition treaty between the UK and the US, which was supposed to be used as a counter-terrorism measure, is widely seen in the UK as one-sided, with the US authorities merely required to make an allegation rather than present a prima facie case.

David Carruthers, CEO of online betting firm BETonSPORTS, was arrested in 2006 while merely changing planes at Dallas airport. En route from Britain to the company's base in Costa Rica, he was accused of heading a company that accepted unlawful bets on the internet placed by Americans – in other words, racketeering. Carruthers quickly became a cause célèbre for opponents of America's sweeping restrictions on internet gaming, with Democratic Congressman Barney Frank describing his airport arrest as 'one of the most Stalinist things I've ever seen my government do'. Carruthers lost his job at BETonSPORTS; the company citing his inability to perform his 'daily business duties' while in jail as the reason for his dismissal. He'd never physically committed a crime in the USA or the UK. However, in 2010, after living under house arrest in a hotel in Missouri for over three years, Carruthers agreed to a deal and pleaded guilty to one count of racketeering conspiracy; he was duly sentenced to 33 months in prison.

The UK has also signed up to a treaty between the European Union and the USA, which allows any Member State to issue an arrest warrant for a UK national, wherever they are, based on little more than an allegation. This measure is based on the premise that justice is a level playing field throughout all 28 states of the EU.

Just because an individual is not in the country in which an offence *may* have been committed does not, however, mean they're protected from the authorities. Although countries such as Russia do not normally extradite their nationals, and others restrict extraterritorial jurisdiction to grave offences such as war crimes and piracy, the world is changing. The aggressive regulatory approach adopted by the US and the UK means that not only do companies need to abide by *every* law in *every* jurisdiction in which they operate, they also need to ensure that their employees are complying with the letter of those laws even if their behaviour may not be a criminal offence in their own country. In recent years, a flood of cases has involved people falling foul of international law when they haven't broken laws in their own country.

It took computer hacker Gary McKinnon, who has Asperger's syndrome, over ten years (and seven Home Secretaries) to win the legal battle to stop his extradition to the USA, after he was caught hacking into US military bases. The Americans alleged he'd altered and deleted files at a naval air station not long after 9/11. He said he'd been looking for evidence of UFOs and extraterrestrial technology that could save the environment. The case against him was only dropped when Home Secretary number seven, Theresa May, accepted that McKinnon was 'seriously ill' and stated: 'Mr McKinnon's extradition would give rise to such a high risk of him ending his life that a decision to extradite would be incompatible with Mr McKinnon's human rights.'

The NatWest Three

In November 2001 British businessmen Giles Darby, David Bermingham and Gary Mulgrew, dubbed the NatWest Three, learned that the SEC was investigating Andy Fastow, Enron Corporation's chief financial officer. The Three decided to voluntarily meet with the FSA to discuss their dealings with Fastow. Bermingham later claimed, '[w]e gave [the FSA] everything because we thought we had nothing to hide.'[17]

Four months later, the FSA completed its inquiries without taking any action. However, it passed on the results of its inquiries to the SEC in America, which passed them on to the Department of Justice. According to *The Times*, so detailed was this report that it told the SEC whom to interview and what evidence to collect to secure a conviction. In 2002 the Three were indicted in Texas, in their absence, on seven counts of wire fraud. Arrested in Britain on 23 April 2004, the Three sued the Serious Fraud Office (SFO) in an attempt to force a prosecution in the UK rather than in the US. 'I cannot imagine anyone has taken the SFO to court for not prosecuting them before,' said Bermingham.

After losing a series of high-profile battles in court, the Three were finally extradited to the USA in 2006, where, under a plea agreement, they admitted to persuading NatWest to sell for $1 million its stake in an Enron subsidiary to a Cayman Islands company in which they had a secret financial interest, and then to selling it back to Enron for $20 million and sharing the profits with Fastow. They were each sentenced to 37 months in prison. Despite, like Carruthers and McKinnon, never having committed a crime in the USA and never having been prosecuted in the UK, even when their crime was committed against their employer in London, the Three could be charged with wire fraud in the US because communications related to the deal had passed through the US communications system and so became subject to the Foreign Corrupt Practices Act (FCPA).

The reach of the FCPA is vast. Companies become subject to US legislation if they are listed in the USA, have any business dealings with the USA, use dollars for transactions or have passed transactions through the USA, for example as SWIFT payments. And with New

York being a cardinal point in the global economy, the chance of an organisation not engaging in any of the above is small to none. Siemens, a German company, was fined £800 million under the FCPA because it was listed on the New York stock exchange.

Since the financial crash in 2008, the US authorities' pursuit of companies falling foul of the FCPA has become ever more vigorous. Agencies such as the Department of Justice and the SEC aggressively pursue foreign companies for related offences and, thanks to the hefty fines they are able to levy, these agencies have even started to make a profit, giving them access to even greater resources.

In the UK, the Bribery Act 2012 is similar to the FCPA, in that it extends UK jurisdiction to offences committed elsewhere, and imposes measures to prevent bribery in other jurisdictions. Theoretically, if a Canadian parent company employed an agent in Kazakhstan who bribed a local official, the directors of the UK subsidiary could be held liable for failing to prevent the bribe being paid. And as with the FCPA, companies that carry out business in the UK can be prosecuted for offences committed anywhere in the world.

This situation presents problems in regions where bribes are the normal way of doing business. However, the risk of falling foul of extra-territorial jurisdiction usually far outweighs the benefits to the business. And it's not just bribes and black money that make a company or executive vulnerable. The risk of an executive being held responsible, like David Carruthers, for a company's actions overseas – even if personally unaware that any laws are being broken – is growing all the time. Although this risk can never be eradicated, it can be mitigated. In the UK, the risk of bribery is in the fourth quadrant – an 'unknown known' – but with proper training and compliance policies it can at least be moved to the first quadrant – a 'known known'.

Say, for example, a company headquartered in the UK has a subsidiary in Nigeria that employs an agent who pays a bribe in order to win a contract. The profits of that contract are then transferred to the UK and into the account of the top company. In theory several offences have been committed. First, the bribe-paying Nigerian agent would be guilty under the UK Bribery Act. If the UK board knew about this behaviour or had no policies in place to abolish bribes, it would also have committed an offence, and the funds returned to the UK would be considered the proceeds of a crime and subject to sequester. Being charged with money laundering is an additional possibility.

The first a board may know of such a situation is when the company is raided by the regulator or it receives a written request for information. In this situation, it is imperative that the company marshals its legal, public affairs and PR resources. In an ideal world the company would conduct its own investigation, present itself to the regulator as soon as possible, make voluntary disclosures and ultimately be seen as a good corporate citizen.

But a mistake companies commonly make is to start by sending in the wrong people; rather than approaching specialist investigative lawyers, they rely on their in-house team or their accountants or auditors. Similarly, rather than bringing in PR crisis specialists, they stick with their regular PR firm and in-house PR director. A PR director of a white goods company might be fantastic at selling fridges; however, they're unlikely to be quite so good when the company is being charged with criminal offences.

Companies also need to be aware that anti-trust laws are subject to extraterritorial legislation too. The European Court of Justice ruled that a number of paper manufacturers based in Norway and Finland – which had not yet joined the EU – were nonetheless subject to EU competition law because their actions outside the EU had an effect on competition within the EU. The so-called 'effects doctrine' means that, although the behaviour was legal in the companies' home countries, it was an infringement of the law in the countries with which they traded.

Conducting business over the internet presents its own problems too. David Carruthers was prosecuted because his company failed to prevent Americans from placing bets online. Yahoo was taken to court in France over the sale of Nazi memorabilia; even though the website was in English and the price for the memorabilia was in dollars, the French judge held that, because the site could be accessed in France, it was in breach of French law, and thus ordered Yahoo to prevent internet users in France from accessing the web page in question.

It's well-nigh impossible for companies to account for every law in every country in which a site can be accessed or to keep on top of every law in every country in which they and their subsidiaries do business. Four main strategies can be used, however, for dealing with the minefield of extraterritorial legislation. First, never underestimate the new, vocal and very public power of the regulators policing activities beyond their borders. Second, pick the most stringent jurisdiction the company operates under and stick to it all over the world. The company may lose some competitive advantage, but it drastically reduces the financial and reputational risk of being prosecuted. Third, implement a uniform compliance system but, in local jurisdictions where the laws might be a bit lighter, adjust accordingly in terms of 'we can do this, we can't do that and we might have to be careful about the other'. Fourth, if a crisis occurs try to blame it on a rogue employee who has clearly disregarded internal compliance measures.

Obviously, the fourth and final strategy is extremely risky and can often backfire spectacularly, as in the case of Siemens, which we will examine in the next chapter.

CHAPTER 4

Rogue employees: The threat from within

It takes 20 years to build a reputation and five minutes to ruin it. If you think about that, you'll do things differently.

Warren Buffett

ON THE MORNING OF 15 NOVEMBER 2006 IN MUNICH, SIX GERMAN POLICE officers and a prosecutor knocked on the door of Reinhard Siekaczek, a 57-year-old sales manager at German engineering giant Siemens' telecommunications division. They held a warrant for his arrest. At the same time, 200 other officers were sweeping into Siemens' headquarters in Munich and over 30 offices and homes of current and former Siemens employees. Siekaczek, a loyal Siemens employee for nearly 40 years, found himself at the centre of one of the largest and highest-profile global corruption scandals in recent times. And he wasn't surprised. 'I know what this is about,' said Siekaczek, as the police filed in. 'I have been expecting you.'[18]

Siekaczek was accused of using his division to mastermind a comprehensive system of slush funds and front firms to hide illegal money transfers, better known as bribes, to win lucrative overseas contracts for Siemens.

The scandal quickly became a crisis that shook Siemens, and led to investigations in more than a dozen countries and cash handouts totalling an estimated €1.3 billion. As soon as the story hit the headlines, Siemens senior executives immediately distanced themselves from Siekaczek, declared their ignorance of his actions and cast him as a rogue employee who had been operating independently of company rules on his own warped initiative.

Siemens was applying the accepted definition of a rogue employee – one who is disloyal, acts against the interests of the company for their own benefit or takes revenge for perceived injustices. In contrast, an employee who challenges the company on ethical grounds is generally called a whistleblower. Closer examination of these terms, however, reveals far more complex reasons for their existence and, consequently, the potential for far more damaging fallout for companies who fail to either understand or challenge the assumptions behind them and prepare accordingly.

Make no mistake, the media loves a juicy high-profile 'rogue' story; from the original rogue trader Nick Leeson (as he now proudly calls himself on his website) through to the more recent cases of Jessica Harper (the head of fraud and security at Lloyds TSB who submitted false invoices to claim approximately £2.4 million for herself and her family) and Christopher Grierson (the senior and highly successful partner at law firm Hogan Lovells who submitted false expenses to the order of £1.27 million to fund his lavish lifestyle) and 32-year-old equities trader Kweku Adoboli, a rising star in the UK investment banking arm of Swiss bank UBS, whose off-the-book activities cost fellow traders their jobs, prompted the resignation of the chief executive and wiped £2.7 billion ($4.5 billion) from the UBS share price.

All too frequently, after a company has become the focus of a scandal, the first line of defence has been to release a statement prepared by a lawyer exonerating the top brass, and then to shove a company spokesperson blinkingly into the media spotlight to claim that said wrongdoing was the sole preserve of one employee – a bad apple; nobody else in the barrel is tainted; the foundations of the barrel remain strong; and, most importantly, nobody above the rank of cleaner had any idea of what was going on. 'The deeds of this bad apple in no way represent the values of our great company' is how a typical statement runs. 'Our long-established traditions of honesty and integrity speak for themselves and in no way could we have anticipated this scandalous course of events. We condemn the actions of this wrongdoer – who no longer works for us – and, after a rigorous internal enquiry, look forward to regaining the trust of our stakeholders/the general public/the SEC.'

Professor Susan Silbey from the Massachusetts Institute of Technology says that the rogue employee defence is dangerous because it disguises the truth that 'a rotten barrel yields rotten apples' and is a blatant attempt to deny flaws in the system and culture that spawned the bad acts in the first place.[19] This was certainly true of the culture at Siemens. For a start, until 1999, bribes were deductible as business expenses under the German tax code, and bribing foreign officials in pursuit of contracts was not a criminal offence.

According to a complaint filed by the US SEC in December 2008, there were at least 290 projects or individual sales involving business in Venezuela, China, Israel, Bangladesh, Nigeria, Argentina, Vietnam, Russia and Mexico in which Siemens 'employed the mails and other means and instrumentalities of U.S. interstate commerce in order to make bribe payments to foreign government officials'. Siemens bribed wherever it felt the money was needed, paying off officials to help sell power generation equipment in Italy, telecommunications infrastructure in Nigeria, national identity cards in Argentina, telecoms and security contracts in Greece for the Athens Olympic Games and so on – the company identified a total of $1.6 billion in what it called 'questionable payments' from 2000 to 2006. In such an environment, Siemens officials subscribed to a basic rule in pursuing business abroad: it played by local rules. 'Paying provisions and bribes was customary in practically all business units of Siemens,' said Reinhard Siekaczek, in a later interview with PBS Frontline, 'except the business units that dealt with lamps and such.' And according to Mark Pieth, chairman of the working group on bribery at the Organisation for Economic Co-operation and Development (OECD), it wasn't even subtle. 'There was no complex financial structuring such as you would find among drug smugglers or money launderers,' he said. 'People felt confident that they were doing nothing wrong.'[20] Between 2001 and 2004 some $67 million in cash was simply carted off in suitcases. Mr Siekaczek later told the court in Munich that the slush funds he set up were 'relatively simple' and 'no great art'.[21]

Even after 1999, when Germany banned corrupt payments to foreign officials, and Siemens shares were listed on the New York stock exchange making it subject to the US Foreign Corrupt Practices Act in 2001, Siemens kept on building the barrel.

Court documents revealed that, of the more than $1.4 billion in illegal payments made by Siemens from 2001 to 2007, Siekaczek's unit was responsible for more than $800 million. Each year, managers in his unit set aside approximately $40–50 million for the payment of bribes. In Greece, Siemens budgeted $10–15 million a year, with bribes in other states as high as 40 per cent of overall contract costs in especially corrupt countries. Typically, amounts ranged from 5 to 6 per cent of a contract's value. The most common method of bribery involved hiring an outside 'consultant' to help 'win' a contract. This consultant was typically a local with ties to ruling leaders. Siemens paid a fee to the consultant, who in turn delivered the cash to the ultimate recipient.

The initial response on the part of the managers in Siekaczek's group to the possibility of a crackdown was neither to respond quickly and publicly nor to bring in external consultants and come clean to the authorities. Rather, they chose to makes its bribery procedures more difficult to detect; in fact, senior managers began using removable sticky notes to authorise potentially incriminating documents. 'The signatories could elegantly remove signs of their involvement if it came to an investigation,' said Siekaczek.

Although Siekaczek claimed he was reluctant to become briber-in-chief – 'I was not the man responsible for bribery ... I organized the cash'[22] – he still justified the practice as an economic necessity. If Siemens didn't continue to pay bribes, it would lose contracts to its competitors and its employees might lose their jobs. In other words, he was not guided by greed or personal advantage but by loyalty and a skewed sense of morality. 'We thought we had to do it,' he said. 'Otherwise, we'd ruin the company.'

Turning a scandal into a crisis
The first inklings of a potential scandal began to appear after the discovery of accountancy errors and 'missing millions', which the Siemens management board, instead of taking the opportunity to come clean, promptly played down as a matter of 'a few million euros'. Later, even as its own estimate of the sums involved spiralled to €420 million (£350 million), key executives continued to claim that the wrongdoing was confined to Siekaczek and his unit and to deny either awareness or involvement.

Heinrich von Pierer, who in the critical years from 2000 to 2006 was at the top of the tree first as CEO of the management board, then as chairman of the supervisory board, refused to step down, claiming he only learned much of the detail of the scandal through the press. He protested that Siemens was not comparable to a medium-sized company where the boss knows on Friday night how much money is in the till. 'We have 30 million bookings a day, at tops 50 million. You cannot expect the CEO to have every detail in mind.' Casting himself as the victim of a media 'big game hunt', he continued to plead ignorance in his memoir, *GipfelStürme* (*Summit Storms*); 'In what way should I have taken responsibility for events that I didn't know about?' he wrote. Eventually forced from office, Pierer continued to insist he had done nothing wrong. 'Despite its outstanding business performance, Siemens had run into a difficult situation due to the in part apparent and in part alleged misconduct of a number of managers and employees,' he said, firmly batting the responsibility back down the line. He then added, nobly: 'The sole reason for my decision today is to serve the best interests of Siemens.'

Following his departure, Pierer sent an email to Siemens employees stating: 'The precarious situation in which our company has found itself, despite excellent business development, has greatly affected me ... the general rush to judgement in the media ... often had no consideration for the facts.'

Nevertheless the facts shamed Siemens and the debacle caused massive reputational damage, not only in the eyes of furious shareholders and investors but also the German public. Siemens' long-held reputation for trustworthiness and integrity was demolished, as was, eventually, the status of senior leaders who tolerated such practices. Presiding judge Peter Noll later described Siemens as operating 'a system of organised irresponsibility that was implicitly condoned'.[23] One German investigator, Uwe Dolata, even went so far as to say 'bribery was Siemens' business model'.[24]

Accounting the accountants

When Siemens' auditor, the German branch of accounting firm KPMG, was investigated for ignoring corrupt payments, it also denied any wrongdoing. Even when investigations revealed hundreds of employees siphoning millions of euros into phoney consultants, false bills and 'shell firms' to pay massive bribes to win contracts, KPMG Germany merrily signed off on Siemens' books *and* the adequacy of its internal controls (according to the company's 2005 filing with the US Securities and Exchange Commission), and were handsomely paid for doing so.

'Usually, experienced KPMG auditors would deliberately ignore suspicious transactions,' said Mr Kutschenreuter, CFO in the telecom equipment unit, while imprisoned as a suspect.[25] Like Siekaczek, Kutschenreuter co-operated fully with the prosecutors and stated that a young KPMG Germany employee in 2004 raised concerns about suspicious payments linked to consultant contracts, and even included them in a letter to Siemens' supervisory board, the German equivalent of a board of directors.

According to Kutschenreuter, the young auditor's concerns were suppressed after a private meeting between Heinz-Joachim Neubürger, Siemens' chief financial officer at the time, and a senior KPMG Germany executive. A few days later, another senior KPMG executive apologised for the 'over-enthusiasm' of the junior auditor.

It wasn't until much later that KPMG changed its mind, conceding in another SEC filing that, having looked at them again, Siemens' controls were not up to scratch. Yet, even while admitting that failure, KPMG continued to deny wrongdoing and claimed it fulfilled its annual auditing obligations at Siemens. It refused to reveal more, asserting that 'confidentiality agreements' precluded it from answering further questions about its audit work in detail.

The fallout

As early as 2004, Siemens executives told Siekaczek to sign a document stating he had followed the company's compliance rules. He reluctantly signed, was moved to another area of the business, but quit soon after. As legal pressure mounted, he heard rumours that Siemens was setting him up for a fall as a rogue operator. 'On the inside, I was deeply disappointed. But I told myself that people were going to be surprised when their plan failed,' Siekaczek said. 'It wasn't going to be possible to make me the only one guilty because dozens of people in the business unit were involved. Nobody was going to believe that one person did this on his own.'[26]

And they didn't.

The US authorities fined Siemens a record $800 million (£523 million). Siemens also agreed to pay a fine of €395 million (£354 million) to settle a case in Munich, its home town, in recognition of the failure of its former board to fulfil its supervisory duties. Its former telecoms division also fined Siemens €201 million for bribery, bringing Siemens' total costs to €2.5 billion, including €850 million in lawyers' and accountants' fees. The US settlement, after a year of negotiations and plea bargaining, saw Siemens pay the US Department of Justice about $450 million (€350 million) to settle charges of bribery and falsifying corporate books. The SEC received another $350 million (€270 million) on similar charges under the Foreign Corrupt Practices Act. The Department of Justice said it was the biggest case it had ever seen in 'scope and magnitude'. Matthew W. Friedrich, the acting chief of the Justice Department's criminal division, called corruption at Siemens 'systematic and widespread'. Linda C. Thomsen, the SEC's enforcement director, said it was 'egregious and brazen'. Joseph Persichini Jr, the director of the FBI's Washington field office, which led the investigation, called it 'massive, wilful and carefully orchestrated'.[27]

Eventually, in a file presented to the SEC on 11 December 2006 (Form 20-F), Siemens conceded that its 'internal control over financial reporting was not effective as of September 30, 2006' and that there had been 'significant evidence of collusion' at the Telecom-Gear unit, the company's largest, 'to misappropriate funds and abuse authority among certain members of senior management along with others'.

The Siemens case is notable for its enormous scope, the sheer quantities of cash involved and the systematic fervour with which the bribes were deployed. It was also notable for the co-operation between law enforcement agencies on a cross-border basis; a good example of the extraterritoriality that we discussed in the last chapter. German prosecutors opened the Siemens' case in 2005 and shortly after that, in 2006, the American authorities joined in after the SEC noted that Siemens' bribery and other improper payments had a strong US jurisdictional nexus; some of the projects with which the payments were made were approved by Siemens' agents in the USA, financed by the World Bank or the US Export–Import Bank, or were made through US bank accounts, made through US-based intermediaries and/or were discussed in meetings in the USA or in 'mail, email, and fax communications into and out of the United States' (although later Siemens was charged and fined for 'accountancy errors' rather than corruption, so that it could still bid for government jobs in the USA).

This kind of international co-operation is set to increase. New laws introduced in 2010 include the UK Bribery Act and the US Wall Street

Reform and Consumer Protection Act. These measures add complexity to a newly aggressive anti-corruption environment spearheaded by the US Foreign Corrupt Practices Act and the OECD's Anti-Bribery Convention. Together, these overlapping legal frameworks mandate companies to commit to functioning internal anti-corruption compliance regimes. When it comes to corporate responsibility, there's no such thing as abroad.

From crisis comes change – or better late than never
In addition to four international investigations, Siemens announced its own rigorous internal inquiry to be conducted by New York law firm Debevoise & Plimpton, which flagged 65 countries for scrutiny in an internal document, according to the *Wall Street Journal*.[28] Following the eventual departures of then-CEO Klaus Kleinfeld and chairman Heinrich von Pierer, the board hired Peter Löscher, the first outsider to become the company's top leader and, in keeping with Rule 3 (When a crisis happens, bring in external consultants), although a little late, appointed Michael Hershman, co-founder of Transparency International, to serve as its adviser – a shrewd move to affiliate itself with a leading anti-corruption expert.

In getting to grips with Rule 4 – To prevent future recurrence, change the culture as well as the policies – Peter Löscher promptly announced a month-long amnesty for employees to come forward and reveal what they knew – from which he explicitly excluded former directors. Around 40 whistleblowers gave evidence, which extended the scandal's reach even further into the boardroom and leading to two of its former executives – Ulrich Bock and Stephan Singer – receiving the largest-ever civil penalties in a corporate foreign bribery case, $524,000 each. Bock was also fined approximately $414,000 in 'disgorgement and interest' too. The *Wall Street Journal* reported that the penalty and disgorgement amounts recommended by the SEC resulted from the executives' unresponsiveness and 'utter refusal to accept any responsibility for their actions'.[29]

Peter Löscher then rolled out strict new rules and anti-corruption/compliance processes. Siemens hired over 500 full-time compliance officers (up from just 86 in 2006), and a former Interpol official to head its new investigation unit. It set up compliance hotlines, and an external ombudsman based worldwide and online.

Siemens launched for its employees a comprehensive training and education programme on anti-corruption practices. By 2008 the company had trained more than half of its 400,000-strong global workforce on anti-corruption issues. Siemens also announced that it would avoid competing in certain known corruption or unethical practice hotspots, such as Sudan – a simple gesture, although not materially punishing to the company's finances. More substantial was the decision to voluntarily suspend its applications for funding from the World Bank for two years. It also agreed to a 15-year programme to pay $100 million to non-profit organisations fighting corruption. Löscher replaced Siemens' bogglingly complex matrix structure with a more streamlined version comprising of just three divisions whose managing directors sit on the management board. Finally, millions of bank account statements, documents and transactions were reviewed and the firm took over 900 internal disciplinary actions, including dismissals. Löscher, widely commended for his desire to end corruption, maintained that changing a corporate culture from one driven solely by the need for success to one driven also by ethical standards 'is a marathon for us, not a sprint'.[30]

Overall, the scandal cost Siemens €2.5 billion, including €2 billion in fines. The firm was also barred from dealings with certain clients. The cost to employees in terms of two years of shame and intense public scrutiny, especially in Germany, where soul-searching and shame are a national pastime, is difficult to calculate.

The Siemens case is significant because it exemplifies two extremes: how not to, and then much later, how to correctly, deal with a crisis. After some blundering mis-steps at the beginning, the company eventually came up with an effective response, which can serve as a blueprint for others in a similar situation. Usually when companies survive it is because they have come clean, rather than waited to be caught. Not only does approaching the regulators before being called by them look good and seem conciliatory, it has the advantage of making a leniency deal more likely. Alternatively, gathering evidence provides space to defend the charges to the hilt. In Siemens' case, as a reward for being *very* co-operative with the SEC, it was eventually charged with the lesser offence of 'accountancy errors' rather than outright corruption.

None of the workers in the barrel was truly rogue; they believed they were loyal to the company, and were putting into effect company policy, even if that policy was at odds with the changes in German law and at the cost of adherence to international law. It was company policy that was rogue – they were just good Germans, labelled 'rogue' to protect the company, when in fact the company itself needed to change.

Kweku Adoboli didn't set out to harm his company, or undermine its stated values either. But incentivised to take risks, and left unchecked by poor management systems, he slipped unnoticed into rogue territory, and then kept slipping.

Kweku Adoboli and UBS

> We were told you wouldn't know where the limit of the boundary was until you got a slap on the back of the wrist. We found the edge, we fell off and I got arrested.
>
> *Kweku Adoboli*

Kweku Adoboli had been working as a trader at UBS's global synthetic equities branch, buying and selling exchange-traded funds when he committed the biggest fraud in British history, which resulted in losses of £1.4 billion. Starting as an analyst in the administrative 'back office' of the investment arm, Adoboli was, by all accounts, a bright, enthusiastic ambitious worker and it took him just two years to gain promotion to trader. And it was his time behind the scenes that laid the groundwork for his fraud, affording him both the ways and means to hide it from his superiors.

Prelapsarian are the days of the small investment bank in which all the partners knew each other personally and new additions to the team were carefully nurtured and watched over in a paternalist fashion. The modern financial services sector does not lend itself to that sort of behaviour.

The relatively anonymous Adoboli found it easy to use the bank's money to place unauthorised trades – essentially bets – on stock markets in November 2008. In many cases he employed simple delaying tactics such as extending the time in which some trades would complete in order to buy himself time to make up any losses. Elsewhere he failed to hedge these unauthorised trades, which, had it worked, would have maximised profits and helped cover his losses, but when it didn't, exposed the bank to greater and greater losses. It was the traditional downward spiral of the unchecked gambler; chasing losses by taking bigger and bigger risks, resulting in bigger and bigger losses, which led to bigger and bigger risks.

And having worked in the operations back rooms Adoboli knew how to cover his tracks. From delaying tactics, he progressed to altering financial records, manipulating processes and, by using 'umbrella accounts', managed to hide his disastrous trades for more than two years, even inventing fictitious counterparties to his trades. In doing so, he was following exactly the same path as Nick Leeson, a back office boy who became a trader and had bankrupted Barings 14 years earlier.

Adoboli's job was meant to be fairly mechanical – hedging positions to reduce the risk of his desk – but it was just far too easy for him to escape the shackles of his pay grade. According to Tracey McDermott, the FSA's director of enforcement and financial crime:

> UBS's systems and controls were seriously defective. UBS failed to take reasonable care to organise and control its affairs responsibly and effectively, with adequate risk management

systems, and failed to conduct its business from the London Branch with due skill, care and diligence. As a result, Adoboli, a relatively junior trader, was allowed to take vast and risky market positions, and hide his activities with ease.[31]

Adoboli never set out to commit fraud, and indeed claimed everything he'd done was aimed at helping the bank, where he viewed his colleagues as 'family'. During his trial he clearly pointed the blame upstairs, and claimed he'd been doing well until, under pressure from senior managers, he changed his risk-avoiding conservative position to a risk-seeking aggressive approach.

During his trial, however, it soon emerged that, despite a six-figure salary, Adoboli's personal financial life was in crisis, and not only did he use payday loans but he'd also accumulated spread-betting losses of £123,000. Sasha Wass, the lead prosecutor, called Adoboli arrogant, reckless and an 'accomplished liar' who 'played God' with the bank's money to boost his ego and wallet through larger bonuses. Sentencing Adoboli, Mr Justice Keith told the trader, perhaps rather obviously, 'There is a strong streak of the gambler in you.'

However temperamentally unsuited to his position, Adoboli, in his own mind, had tried his best, had only done wrong to further the interests of the business; he even went so far as to tell the jurors that he was loyal to UBS 'until they called the police'. And, although he was working alone, he was clearly helped in his crime. First, by the complexity of over-the-counter derivatives themselves, which instead of dispersing or balancing risk (hedging), as was widely claimed by such former luminaries as Alan Greenspan ('complex financial products ... have significantly lowered the costs of, and expanded the opportunities for, hedging risks'[32]), merely pushed it underground. Exchange-traded funds (ETFs) had grown in popularity and, as they did so, had become particularly exotic and opaque as a means of pursuing assets with above-average returns. Second, by the so-called 'agency risk', as warned against by Adam Smith; that is, the increasing separation of control and ownership – in other words, gambling with *other* people's money. Third, by a remuneration system – common across the financial sector but also in many others – that compensated traders for the size of a trade and not its long-term outcome. Lastly, by UBS's own auditing and compliance systems and controls – or lack of them.

Much to the chagrin, and ultimately to the cost, of UBS, their controls failed to pick up the huge losses Adoboli had generated, and he was never actually caught. He handed himself in and told all, thus making the unusual leap from rogue employee to whistleblower. Sending what became known as the 'bombshell email' to William Seward, an accountant at UBS, under the subject heading 'An Explanation of my Trades', Adoboli admitted that his ETF trades '[were] not trades that I have done with a counterparty as I previously described'; rather, they were made to suppress the losses he had accrued through off-book trades. He went on to claim that, while his trades initially made money, the losses mounted as the eurozone crisis escalated.

'Initially I had been short futures through June and those lost money when the first Greek confidence vote went through in mid June,' he wrote. 'Although I had a couple of opportunities to unwind the long trade for a negligible loss, I did not move quickly enough.' He then continued, with more prescience than he had demonstrated while trading, 'I take full responsibility for my actions and the shit storm that will now ensue … I am deeply sorry to have left this mess for everyone and to have put my bank and my colleagues at risk.'

Adoboli was young and relatively lowly when he went off the rails. But rogue employees – whether intentional or unintentional, feckless or malicious – have been found at all levels of corporate operation. The challenge for senior management is recognising how to predict who, when and under what circumstances rogue employees might appear. Then, should the worst happen, they must have appropriate strategies in place that allow them to respond quickly and effectively. For no set of compliance policies and systems, however bulletproof they may seem, will protect an organisation from those who deliberately set out to circumvent them. Bear in mind that, if incentive schemes reward certain behaviours and punish others, compliance can quickly become a matter of spin and sophistry. When the Blair government wanted to end the practice of leaving patients on trolleys in NHS hospital corridors, it employed a system of financial penalties. In response, managers removed the wheels from trolleys and reclassified them as beds. When targets and policies are imposed by a distant central authority, all too frequently deceit is the response at ground level, as individuals attempt to find the best way to circumvent compliance.

The only way is ethics

A recent paradigm shift in modern business involves the setting up of specialist legal compliance departments. Instead of compliance being the responsibility of the board, CEO, senior partner and so on, that function is often now outsourced and its associated responsibility devolved to a third force within the organisation. Again, we see the law of unintended consequences at work. The company's intent is to demonstrate that compliance to regulations is so important that it deserves a dedicated departmental structure all of its own. However, once the compliance department has been set up, other departments may conclude that the responsibility for staying inside the rules belongs elsewhere; compliance is now someone else's problem. Creating a separate compliance function risks separating compliance from the company's day-to-day activities.

Enshrining compliance in a separate function, technically speaking, may relieve executives from certain legal responsibilities. But in the court of public opinion those at the top are still held responsible for the organisations they are seen to be running, even though the scale of these organisations is far too large to fall within a single person's ambit. The question 'what did you know and when did you know it?' can no longer be sent to the corner unanswered. The sight of senior executives being publicly grilled on TV by government committees has become far more commonplace in recent times.

For compliance policies to be effective, they need to be clear, sincere, transparent and taught. Identification of compliance assessment areas (mapping) is the first step. If a company does not know what to measure, it does not understand its vulnerability and it cannot control it. And if a company cannot control vulnerability, it cannot improve its performance. Siemens radically restructured its organisational hierarchy and simplified its compliance programmes to reduce the responsibility gap between the top and the bottom of the company. There should be no scope for managers to establish a corrupt culture and then inculcate those beneath them. Emerging rogues would not only become visible faster, but the procedures to report concerns would also be easier and less fraught with consequence. The traditional corporate response to those who reported on junior members of staff was to pat them on the head; those who reported on more senior staff were fired.

Compliance policies tend to be revised and strengthened after the event – closing the stable door after the horse has bolted. Some firms attempt to take a proactive approach, aiming to spot potential offenders before they actually undertake any wrongdoing. This approach usually takes the form of employee testing as part of the HR process. Techniques range from tentatively scientific psychological profiling, all the way through to more dubious methods such as handwriting analysis and astrology.

Sometimes even the most diligent psychometric testing can result in epic failures. After calling Paul Flowers, then CEO of the Co-operative Bank, a 'financial illiterate' after he'd revealed that he had no idea of the value of the bank's assets (he stated £3 billion when the correct figure was actually £47 billion), Clive Adamson, head of supervision at the Financial Conduct Authority (FCA), asked banking veteran Rodney Baker-Bates why Flowers had beaten him to the job. 'I was told he did very well on the psychometric tests,' he replied. Flowers also had a conviction for gross indecency and had been forced to resign from Bradford council after adult content was found on his computer.

The psychometric tests used by the Co-op Bank were clearly deficient in this case. But amongst all the questionable offerings in this field there are some with established track records of screening out potential bad apples. Some good examples are the Hogan personality profiling system and the CultureMetrics product, developed by John Taylor and Adrian Furnham, which uses a web-based system to track how employees' attitudes change over time.

Whether a rogue employee can be psychologically profiled at all, let alone through a formalised system of HR performance management rules, disciplinary procedures and so on is still a matter of debate. Often the very qualities that make a candidate or employee seem perfect for the job – smart, ambitious, hard-working – are the very characteristics that prove so devastatingly effective when they go rogue. And companies and institutions that promote a culture of 'we're special' and 'we're the best' often have the hardest time admitting that they're not. Alongside punitive measures, the result can be disastrous. When the Soviet economy collapsed, it was doing fantastically well – on paper. For decades, as productivity slumped, managers got round the dangerous prospect of reporting failure by lying. They inflated output figures knowing they would go unchallenged by those above them – who likewise didn't want to be seen as failing in their duty – all the way to the top. Until they ran out of toilet paper. And bread. And everything. The entire system was rogue.

Surprisingly, one of the characteristics of individuals who really are rogue is that, with hindsight, they seem so easy to spot. Bradley Manning, the rogue US intelligence officer who leaked 700,000 secret military documents, had a history of bizarre behaviour that had been reported many times by fellow soldiers before he went rogue; he'd been restrained because other soldiers thought he was trying to grab a weapon, he'd hit a female officer in the face and he'd sent a sergeant a photograph of himself dressed as a woman. But the question of why a clearly unstable man was allowed access to hundreds of thousands of classified files has never really been asked or answered.

And for organisations sailing in new regulation-infested waters, a combination of re-emboldened regulators, a tenacious, self-interested press, class action lawyers representing shareholders who have lost money as a result of corrupt/incompetent practice, 24-hour news coverage and the unpredictable power of social media mean that the wrongdoings of a single rogue employee can be fatal to the business as a whole.

The ubiquitous nature of social media makes companies increasingly vulnerable to the damage that can be caused by rogue employees, as the next section demonstrates.

Domino's Pizza

> We got blindsided by two idiots with a video camera and an awful idea.
>
> *Domino's spokesman, Tim McIntyre*

In April 2009, two Domino's Pizza employees in America, Kristy Hammonds and Michael Setzer, decided it would be fun to make a prank video of themselves at work: they stuck cheese up their nose, put snot on the bread and wiped their bare backsides with a dish sponge. 'In about five minutes it'll be sent out on delivery where somebody will be eating these, yes, eating them, and little [do] they know that [that] cheese was in his nose and that ... some lethal gas ... ended up on their salami,' said one. 'Now that's how we roll at Domino's.'

They posted the video on YouTube and within 24 hours it had amassed over a million views; five of the 12 results on the first page of a Google search for 'Dominos' referred to the clip. Discussions about Domino's spread throughout Twitter, and the collective 'eeeeuw' would soon be heard on the New York stock exchange.

And Domino's said nothing – for 48 hours.

Domino's spokesman, Tim McIntyre, later explained that the

reason executives took so long to respond was that they hoped that staying below the radar would mean the controversy would quiet down. Which just proves how little they knew about the social media radar. Others have suggested that their mistake was calling in the lawyers before activating their PR department, and wasting time locating the guilty employees and examining legal options rather than organising an effective response in the media. Either way, during those 48 hours, the crisis turned into a public relations disaster.

The 'Domino effect' was a 10–12 per cent drop in stock value over the next week. 'What we missed was the perpetual mushroom effect of viral sensations,' said McIntyre. And how. Domino's has since developed a social media strategy. A good policy will make it clear to employees that certain forms of online behaviour are not acceptable – such as commenting on the company or revealing sensitive information – and will ask employees to add 'the views on this profile do not represent the views of my employer' should they choose to publicly affiliate themselves with the company.

Domino's is far from the first company to suffer reputational damage with off-script employees. Burger King fired a worker for bathing in a kitchen sink and then posting a video of the deed. The pithily titled 'FedEx Guy Throwing My Computer Monitor Over Fence' – a 20-second security tape of a FedEx employee doing just that – has been viewed over nine million times and was picked up by CNN. 'United Breaks Guitars', a country and western lament by United Airlines customer David Carroll, describing how its baggage handlers broke his guitar and then put him through an 18-month runaround when he sought compensation, has had over 13 million hits and spawned a new career for Mr Carroll – as a consumer advocate.

Not all social media firestorms are a disaster, however. When disgruntled HMV employees took over the company's Twitter account after being sacked by the ailing retailer ('There are over sixty of us being fired at once! Mass execution of loyal employees who love the brand'), the company was made a laughing stock for a day. But no reputational damage occurred and threats to the balance sheet proved non-existent.

Others do blow up without warning, though sometimes from unexpected quarters. When US fast food giant Chick-fil-A's CEO, Dan Cathy, decided to chip in on the debate about gay marriage on a syndicated radio talk show, stating that we are 'inviting God's judgment on our nation when we shake our fist at Him and say: "We know better than you as to what constitutes a marriage"', he created an immediate media firestorm. On the ground, both ardent supporters and angry picketers showed up at the stores. Although Cathy's comments ultimately didn't hurt short-term business – and even helped it – neither Chick-fil-A executives nor its shareholders had been consulted. And at a time when the company was looking to expand beyond its established Southern market into Chicago, New York and Los Angeles, Cathy's comments could have threatened the brand's image and made it harder to reach out to big-city dwellers.

Many insider threats are best handled at the hiring stage. Potential employees (including temporary staff and consultants – and, indeed, CEOs) should be evaluated to identify personality or character weaknesses or a pattern of behaviour that is poorly adapted to the circumstances. For example, a food-preparation business that hires lots of young people who own smartphones should establish a stringent employee training regime, promote an awareness of good practice and point out the consequences of failing to adhere to it, and this should be included in the employment contract. In America, this situation has to be handled with a degree of caution. A fine line exists between telling an employee 'don't bad mouth us on Twitter' and impinging upon their right to free speech. Never underestimate the role of boredom in the rogue behaviour of youth.

The huge increase in the number of young people going on to higher education and the resulting student debt has led to a generation of overqualified young people doing mundane jobs in service industries, flipping burgers as a means to something else. But an ever-changing economy means companies need talented, creative types who can take the initiative and find new ways to do things. If these types of people are trapped in jobs that aren't challenging or stimulating enough, they may turn to rogue activity just for fun. Creating opportunities to absorb the talent of your staff is the most effective way to fend off the minimum-wage prankster.

The first step in dealing with rogue employees is to create a culture in which workers will not feel justified in behaving in such a way. Increasing trust between different levels of employees, particularly between senior management and lower-level staff, is vital for the overall internal security of a company; if no trust is demonstrated, why should it be returned? The mantra of we're all one big happy family doesn't work if workers' emails and blogs are subject to management surveillance, and security cameras are employed in the staffroom. To a resentful unhappy worker, such tactics often provoke retaliation. Treating your employees as responsible adults not naughty children and listening to people's grievances are fundamental elements in an anti-rogue toolbox.

And be fair. Advising employees that their default response to a workplace dispute should be dealing with it internally, through their supervisor or via the HR department, rather than expressing their gripe online is pointless if it's management treatment that they take issue with. Rogue employees often feel they've been unfairly treated, overlooked for promotion, been the victim of a biased reward system, seen others take credit for their work, witnessed the parachuting in of unqualified relatives and seen brown-nosing work. If an organisation's HR processes aren't fair, transparent and objective, it's storing up wood for a future fire, twig by twig. Employees may still grumble but if a company can point to a structured process for promotion and pay based on proper evaluation, they're much less likely to air their grievances outside the company.

Also beware of the management bully. Success isn't the only corporate metric. Managers who always reach their targets, but do so by treating those below them badly, are storing up trouble for the future. Organisations can far too easily become top heavy with alpha managers with a tendency to browbeat more vulnerable underlings. Managers need to receive training in effective employee relations; codes, rules and guidelines are not enough to prevent 'I hate my boss' rogue behaviour.

Hypocrisy in corporate presentation materials can also be a motivating factor. If there is a glaring mismatch between the company's public face and what really goes on, a rogue employee is much more likely to reveal the truth. The bottom line for most companies is that results matter. This is obviously necessary for any company to survive. However, when seeking results means that management pays lip service to business ethics rather than engraining them in company culture, some employees may find it difficult to stomach corporate statements about 'integrity' and 'putting clients first' when they know that such lofty values are not applied to staff. One of the 'known unknowns' for Rumsfeld was that not all US soldiers thought the way he did. Sergeant Joseph M. Darby, an MP at the Abu Ghraib prison, came into possession of the notorious photographs of soldiers torturing prisoners and couldn't remain silent. He agonised for a month before whistleblowing on his friends and handing the photos to the US Army Criminal Investigation Command. 'It violated everything I personally believed in,' he said, 'and all I'd been taught about the rules of war.'

Stop, thief!

The term 'whistleblower' – said to derive from a London Bobby's whistle of alarm in response to a crime – was adopted and popularised by consumer activist Ralph Nader in the early 1970s to replace the negative 'informer' and 'snitch'. It has since become shorthand for anybody drawing attention to illegal or foul play in business and government. Or just claiming to.

The first recorded corporate whistleblower was Stanley Adams, a senior executive at Hoffman–La Roche. In 1973 he revealed to EEC regulators that his company was price fixing in the vitamin market. Unfortunately for him, however, the EEC regulators revealed his name, which resulted in his arrest by the Swiss government on a charge of industrial espionage. He spent six months in jail (not an auspicious start for whistleblowing). Attitudes toward whistleblowing have evolved considerably during the past 50 years. Where loyalty to the company was once the norm, public outrage regarding corporate misconduct has now created a more fertile ground for whistleblowing. The passing of the Sarbanes–Oxley Act in 2002 and other laws protecting whistleblowers means that management now has to monitor reputational risk, internally and externally, as diligently as any other corporate risk. According to recent research into whistleblowing carried out by the University of Greenwich in conjunction with Public Concern at Work,[33] whistleblowers demonstrate loyalty and a desire to see their company live up to its values. Consider these facts:

- 83 per cent of whistleblowers raise the alarm at least twice, usually internally.
- 15 per cent of whistleblowers, only, raise a concern externally.
- 74 per cent of whistleblowers say nothing is done about the wrongdoing.
- 60 per cent of whistleblowers receive no response from management, negative or positive.
- 19 per cent of whistleblowers experience formal action (disciplinary or demotion) in response to their actions.
- 15 per cent of whistleblowers are dismissed.

It's often said that there is no good way of getting a divorce, no good way of dying and no good way of whistleblowing. The evidence shows that the crucial factor is not the method of disclosure, but how the disclosure is received.

Firestone and the Ford tyre controversy

> At Firestone, nothing is more important to us than the safety of our customers.
>
> *Gary Crigger, Executive Vice President, Firestone Inc., 2000*

Alan Hogan was a factory floor worker at a Firestone tyre plant in North Carolina when he saw a picture of an 18-year-old in a newspaper. Daniel Van Etten, a high school student and promising young football player from West Virginia University, had died in a car accident. The paper carried a photo of the vehicle's tyres and, the moment he saw them, Hogan *knew* why the tread had peeled away from the steel ply like skin from a banana. Because he helped make them.

The Ford Explorer and Firestone tyre fiasco caused 1,400 car accidents and hundreds of deaths, and is destined to take its place in the textbooks among the most celebrated examples of bungled public relations. Not only did it fail every single point in crisis management, it repeated these mistakes again and again and again. In 1997, the same year as the Van Etten accident, a singing-teacher's car flipped over after a blowout had caused her to lose control of the vehicle. Her husband died and both her legs were amputated below the knee. A mother driving on a motorway in Texas with her two boys was killed instantly when the tyres popped off her SUV. Cynthia Jackson and her husband were driving along when a tyre peeled off one of the back wheels and the car rolled. Her husband also died and she lost both legs. Barbara Haffey's Explorer rolled over after a tyre malfunction and her husband, who was in the front passenger seat, died. Jose Juan Menendez and Clotilde Menendez were killed in Florida following a tyre blowout. Timothy Lockwood was on his way to a meeting when a rear tyre on his Explorer blew, causing the vehicle to roll over. His neck was broken and he suffocated to death.

Ignoring the signals

Internal documents later revealed a Ford Saudi dealer had sent a concerned letter to Firestone regarding the tyres' propensity to blow out. However, as the accident reports began to mount up, rather than announcing a product recall and conducting an urgent enquiry – as advised by its PR firm – Firestone took a lawyer-driven approach and insisted that its tyres were safe. It even went one further and actually blamed the victims for causing the accidents by either driving badly or overinflating the tyres. This strategy proved disastrous. Dispirited, Firestone's PR firm quit.

In 1999 Ford began quietly replacing Firestone tyres on Explorers sold in Saudi Arabia, making no mention of safety concerns; it called the replacement programme a 'customer notification enhancement action'. In the USA, with its lawyers raring to go, Firestone threatened a local news organisation that had begun sniffing around the story, accusing them of spreading 'falsehoods and misrepresentations that improperly disparage Firestone and its product, the Radial ATX model tire'. Displayed on the news organisation's website, Firestone's letter may go some way to explaining why no other news outlet picked up the story for some time.

Disgusted by what he saw as company lies, Hogan went public, and revealed to the media Firestone's reckless disregard for safety and cost-cutting attempts to reuse otherwise useless material. He described the use of 'dry stock', a combination of no-longer-tacky steel belts and rubber. Workers placed it in a storage area called the 'bank' and then used it in production by utilising illegal tricks such as gluing the tyres to the steel. He also saw oil, water, cigarette butts, finger tape, chunks of hardened rubber, and metal or wood shavings mixed with the tyre stock, padding out supposedly A1 rubber. Hogan said workers were under intense pressure to meet quotas and making faulty tyres had become a matter of routine.

Hogan wasn't after fame. He wasn't after money. Unlike Firestone's executives and lawyers, he felt bad about being involved in a process that harmed innocent people. In response to Hogan's disclosures, Firestone's lawyers again went on the offensive, publicly disparaging his reputation, and, because he'd left the company by that time, portraying him as a disgruntled ex-employee. It didn't work; Hogan stayed put.

Whistleblowers tend not to be weak-willed; if they were, they wouldn't come forward in the first place. In many regards Hogan was luckier than most in that he had transferable skills and was able to set up his own body shop repairs business. White-collar workers all too often find it impossible to regain employment in their chosen field once they've been tarnished with the soubriquet whistleblower.

How organisations have traditionally dealt with whistleblowers also presents a dismal picture. Apart from outright dismissal, acts of retaliation can include demotion, bogus complaints about job performance, random reassignment and relocation, forced psychological examinations, investigation of an employee's finances and personal life, whispering campaigns and generally making the job difficult. When an employee's pension and, in the USA, health insurance are tied to their contract, threats of cancellation and financial ruin are commonplace. 'The menu of reprisals is limited only to the imagination,' says Thomas Devine,[34] legal director of the Government Accountability Project (GAP), a Washington-based public-interest watchdog group that represents both government and corporate whistleblowers. According to Dr Rita Pal, who exposed patient neglect in the NHS,

> The pariah effect makes you essentially unemployable, due to the perceptions people have. I do have regrets on occasion when I look at the personal consequences. I am a human being after all and the devastation to my life has been incredible. The hardship for a whistleblower is hard to cope with. The worst aspect is that few people understand that vulnerability and there is little by way of support.[35]

In Hogan's case, company attorneys scrutinised his work and his family life. An anonymous fax, which was later traced to Firestone's accounts office, told workers not to do business with anyone who patronised Hogan's new business.

In May 2001, shortly after Hogan's testimony, Firestone finally announced the biggest tyre recall in history. Still not getting the point, it also explained that the complaints it had received about faulty tyres hadn't raised any 'red flags' because in relative terms, considering how many it sold, few tyres had actually failed. The National Highway Traffic Safety Administration (NHTSA) reported a total of 148 deaths and 525 injuries involving Firestone tyres. The Middle East (where Firestone claimed the hot weather had caused the tread separation) counted seven deaths and Venezuela forty-six.

If Firestone had established effective feedback loops that would have allowed Hogan to report his misgivings to authorities that would listen without his running the risk of being fired or labelled a snitch, the company would have saved itself several billions of dollars, maintained its reputation and gained an iconic place in American industrial folklore. And people needn't have died.

And had Firestone dealt with the media – disclosing what it knew and when it knew it – or presented itself to the NHTSA, or hired outside examiners to report to a regulatory body, it may, as Siemens did, have laid out a path for recovery and rehabilitation. But it didn't. And it cost the company billions. In fact, Ford/Firestone cases are still being settled. 'In the beginning, I did all this for the Van Ettens,' said Hogan. 'As it blew up, it turns out I just inadvertently helped a lot of other people. That's kind of humbling.'

As badly handled cases go, Firestone was a corker. But companies consistently make similar mistakes when confronted with a whistleblower's revelations. First, like Firestone, rather than bringing in a PR company to deal *with* the media rather than to stonewall or threaten it, and genuinely independent lawyers and financial investigators to go through the books, companies often try to get away with conducting the investigation themselves, often via their HR department and using friendly lawyers such as those who draw up their corporate deals for them. Sometimes this approach is justified by cost considerations; after all, investigations don't come cheap. Not upsetting the workforce is another claim – investigations can be disruptive and create worker unease. But rarely is an internal investigation ever seen by the outside world as anything other than disingenuous and self-serving. Whitewashes rarely work, and can even make a company look grubbier. The original investigation into *News of the World* staff misconduct, for example, ordered and paid for by News Corp, was carried out by a law firm with a very limited remit and widely seen as an attempt by the company to minimise, and conceal by omission, what was obviously a massive and unheeded problem. When further investigations revealed the extent of such illegal behaviour, public outrage resulted in the tabloid's closure.

Sometimes, even external advisors can be seen as biased by the workforce, employed by the company brass to protect the corporate structure by throwing junior employees under the bus. Obviously, not only is this bad for employee morale, but a disgruntled ex-employee can do as much damage as an employed one – maybe even more as they have less to lose. For any investigation to work, it must not only be impartial, it must be seen to be impartial. Otherwise, a company has no chance of staying ahead of the game.

HBOS

> Not so much a cautionary tale [as] a manual of bad banking.
> *Parliamentary Commission on Banking Standards*

HBOS collapsed in 2008, wiping out 96 per cent of shareholder value, costing thousands of jobs and forcing a £20.5 billion bailout on the part of the taxpayer. The Banking Standards Commission later said former bosses Sir James Crosby, Andy Hornby and Lord Stevenson were guilty of a 'colossal failure' of management. HBOS' aggressive over-expansion, poor risk controls, complacent management and a narcoleptic regulator all but destroyed a bank with a market capitalisation of £40 billion. And it did not go unnoticed. One man saw it coming and was perfectly placed. As head of group risk at HBOS, Paul Moore warned the HBOS board – as 83 per cent of whistleblowers do, he did so internally – that the bank was 'going too fast' and 'was a serious risk to financial stability and consumer protection', as he later revealed to a Treasury Select Committee.

He was loyal, diligent and doing his job. And he was sacked. But simply getting rid of a dissenter, without addressing the underlying concerns for dissent, doesn't make the problem go away. Just the person pointing to it. Often, when people refer to the emperor's new clothes, they make it a tale about childish wisdom, whereas what the story is really about is power. Luckily for the boy, it was a Danish story; if he'd tried it in Russia in the 1950s or in China under Mao, not only would he have been killed, but his family would've been rounded up too. Today's corporate reactions are less severe, but none the less swingeing. No one likes to be called naked. Moore was lucky to be merely fired.

Before a parliamentary commission on banking standards, Moore said that HBOS executives threatened anybody who questioned the bank's phenomenal risk-taking. 'When I tried to resolve the previous difficulties with Jo Dawson [who replaced Moore as group risk director], she stood up, pointed at me, and said, "I'm warning you. Don't you make an effin' enemy out of me,"' he said. 'It demonstrated that if a senior executive thought it was perfectly OK to speak to the head of regulatory risk in that tone, you can imagine how the culture spreads through the organisation.'

A gagging clause isn't worth the paper it's written on

Gagging clauses in severance agreements have been used by organisations for decades, but are widely perceived as a nothing more lofty than a strategy to hide failure. The BBC was recently condemned for issuing pay-off deals and using gagging clauses to silence 20 former staff who had left claiming to be victims of bullying or harassment. According to journalist Miriam O'Reilly, staff were instructed 'not to say anything negative about the BBC'.

When Moore turned whistleblower in 2009 he'd also taken a pay-off and signed a confidentiality agreement. But eventually his need to tell the truth outweighed all other concerns. And also, in the time lapse, the truth of his observations had been revealed. 'I took the decision to speak out on the night Lehman Brothers went down. I was breaching a confidentiality agreement but I thought the greatest good for the greatest number of people was to speak up because it would feed into the policy debate,' he said. Before the Treasury Select Committee, Moore stated that it was chief executive Sir James Crosby who took the decision to fire him, he took the decision 'alone' and, having ignored his warnings, continued to steer the company onto the rocks.

In a statement, Sir James, who by then had migrated from HBOS to become deputy chairman of the Financial Services Authority, agreed to step down from that role without being asked. Sensitive to the trials of being on a parliamentary committee, he explained: 'I don't want to make their job any more difficult at a difficult and trying time.' He also claimed that HBOS had 'extensively investigated' Moore's allegations and concluded that they 'had no merit'. He then added, 'I nonetheless feel that the right course of action for the FSA is for me to resign from the FSA board, which I do with immediate effect.'[36] Knighted for services to the financial industry in 2006, he tried to voluntarily return his knighthood; however, it was formally annulled on 6 June 2013.

You can't buy loyalty

Paul Moore wasn't motivated by money. 'Whistleblowers,' he said, 'are raising issues because they care about their company deeply and this is misunderstood as disloyal subversion. Money was never a consideration. ... I was earning hundreds of thousands a year as one of the biggest compliance officers in the country. By comparison, last year I earned £15,000.'[37] But things may be about to change.

A whistleblower from software company Autonomy decided to step forward and tell their new bosses at Hewlett-Packard about alleged financial irregularities in the business. HP has since written off $8.8 billion (£5.5 billion) from the value of Autonomy, which it had bought for $10 billion less than a year earlier, and informed the FBI and Securities and Exchange Commission. As for the anonymous whistleblower, whether or not they could be facing the sack is financially moot; they could be entitled to a multimillion-dollar payout thanks to new rules introduced by the Wall Street regulator that mean a whistleblower is entitled to up to 30 per cent of a fine issued for wrongdoing.

Launched in 2013, the first award saw nearly $50,000 go to a whistleblower who alerted the Securities and Exchange Commission to a multimillion-dollar investment fraud. And the US tax authorities have introduced similar reward schemes. Former UBS banker Bradley Birkenfeld was given $104 million for assisting the US tax authorities with its investigation into the Swiss bank's accounts. Former GlaxoSmithKline employee Cheryl Eckard exposed contamination problems at a pharmaceutical factory in Puerto Rico and a subsequent cover-up by company bosses. She received $96 million under the False Claims Act – her share of the $750 million criminal and civil settlement between US regulators and the firm.

And while there are no state-sanctioned financial incentives for whistleblowers in the UK and the City regulator is unlikely to follow Wall Street's lead – a new survey by risk advisers Kroll discovered UK employees were responsible for nearly 25 per cent of all tip-offs to SEC from overseas workers, suggesting financial incentives in one jurisdiction could entice whistleblowers to come forward in another. Benedict Hamilton, managing director at Kroll, said: 'We have already seen a sharp rise in whistleblowing tip-offs to the regulator in the last few years and the offer of rewards would almost certainly accelerate this trend.'

The threat posed by whistleblowers and rogue employees will never go away. Some employees will always get bored; some will still follow orders even if they're illegal and then resent carrying the can later. Others will believe they're doing the right thing by the company – whatever the law or public opinion says. And there will always be those who feel morally motivated, reporting wrongdoing to their superiors and, if that doesn't work, going outside the company. Rogue employees and whistleblowers rarely come out of the blue. Most are smouldering rather than sudden, and are the result of mistakes made by management.

Organisations are subjected to ever-increasing scrutiny from above by regulators and from below by a general public able to broadcast its opinions via social media. These developments make the threat posed by rogue employees and whistleblowers more potent. The way in which companies are being squeezed between these two forces is the subject of our next chapter.

CHAPTER 5

The rock and the whirlpool

IF AN EMPLOYEE COMMITS A CRIME, THEY SHOULD GO TO PRISON. END OF story. But towards the latter part of the twentieth century, this view began to change. It was no longer the end of the story. This was best illustrated when Nick Leeson bankrupted Barings bank in 1995. Leeson was a crook. He deliberately and repeatedly broke the law and then covered his tracks with fraudulent record-keeping in order to enrich himself. But when the story broke, that was not how it played out in the press. The senior management of Barings, who might have expected some sympathy as victims of the crime, found the finger of blame pointing at them instead. In the eyes of the public, a hardworking 'barrow boy made good' had put one over the 'posh but dim' directors. The board of directors, rather than being victims of the fraud, were seen as culprits as a result of their lax oversight and inadequate systems. They were caught between the rock and the whirlpool: a rising regulatory burden on the one hand and a fickle but opinionated public on the other.

Corporate crises change a lot more than just the company; they also change the environment, the regulatory landscape and public opinion. These are questions we now want to address. Why has the quantity of regulation increased so dramatically in recent times? How is it that the general public, who profess to abhor red tape, is actually responsible for creating so much of it? Will there ever be a time when regulations actually decrease? How do the 'court of law' and the 'court of public opinion' interact with each other? Which of the two is more powerful?

Land of the free?

America is increasingly one of the most heavily regulated countries on earth. The World Economic Forum conducts an annual survey which ranks countries based on the burden of government regulation. Countries with the least red tape come out at the top of the list. In the last seven years, the USA has fallen from 23rd to 80th place. Emerging markets feature at the top of the list, with Singapore in the number one slot and China ranked as 14th. Europe fares particularly badly, with Spain 125th, France 130th, Portugal 132th, Greece 144th and Italy worst of all at 146th. This would seem to suggest a relationship between democracy and regulation; the stronger the democratic institutions, the greater the burden of government regulation.

> Two economists are walking down the street. One says to the other, 'Look! There is a £20 note lying on the pavement.' The other replies, 'You must be mistaken, dear boy. It can't be a £20 note. If it was, market forces dictate that someone would have already picked it up.'

This old joke about economists has at its heart a warning about using the existence of something to prove that there must be a demand for it. Mindful of this warning, we can illustrate the regulatory burden in the USA in a different way. The lobbying industry on Capitol Hill has grown exponentially in the last few decades; from its beginnings in the early 1970s, it has expanded so much that there are now 20 lobbyists for every member of Congress. These lobbyists are paid for by large corporations that, presumably, are getting value for money. The conclusion must be that the potential impact of new regulations on business has dramatically increased in the last 40 years, so much so that it has created a whole new $20 billion industry in the USA: the lobbying industry.

For anyone running a business, this fact will strike a chord. If you do a quick mental survey of all the different departments in a company, every one of them has seen a big increase in government red tape in recent years. Let's start on the factory floor. The growth in health and safety regulations has become legendary. So much so that 'health and safety gone mad' is a favourite newspaper headline. There is no doubt that the intentions of these regulations are good and we have certainly come a long way since the horrors of Victorian child labour. The safety record in dangerous industries such as construction or mining has improved dramatically and saved many lives. But, on the other hand, it is hard not to ridicule the excessive implementation of such rules. Is it really necessary to file a written risk assessment before putting up Christmas decorations in the office? Or to wear safety goggles before putting up a poster with drawing pins? In some offices, visitors are chastised if they do not hold the handrail when walking down the stairs. In others, a cup of coffee cannot be carried around the office without being fitted with the appropriate cover because it is a scalding hazard.

The office environment must not only be safe for employees but also non-discriminatory. Which leads us to the second major area of regulation that has ballooned over the last few decades and the other headline staple of the tabloids, 'political correctness gone mad'. Again, the intentions of this legislation are completely laudable. No one in their right mind would disagree with the principle that everyone should be treated equally regardless of gender, ethnicity or sexual preference. But government attempts to enforce this situation through regulation are, perversely, making the situation worse. It is another example of the unintended consequences that we discussed in Chapter 2. Anti-discrimination legislation is so robust that almost any woman who gets fired will be advised by her lawyer to make a claim of discrimination, which most companies will automatically pay off just to get rid of the problem. The more mess and fuss involved in firing someone, the less likely a company is to hire that person in the first place. When comparing different countries, economists can clearly demonstrate a causal link between inflexible labour markets and higher unemployment. It is a similar mechanism at work among minority employees. So legislation designed to protect minorities can have the unintended consequence of making it more difficult for them to get a job.

So much for the factory floor and the HR department. Let's look at some other areas of corporate activity, such as customers and suppliers. Globalisation has driven an outsourcing revolution that has stretched supply chains over many different countries, each with its own legal environment. This development has introduced new risk and uncertainty into supply chains and a greater possibility of falling foul of extraterritorial legislation. New bribery and corruption legislation has meant that dealing with overseas customers and suppliers is more complicated than previously. Different cultures have different expectations when awarding large contracts and what may appear as a bribe in one context is seen as a finder's fee in another. These situations are complex and navigating the correct ethical route through the moral labyrinth isn't easy.

All in all, the burden of new governmental regulation has had an impact on every part of an organisation. Why has it grown so much? One important catalyst for the introduction of new legislation is the impact of a corporate crisis. The Enron scandal triggered the passing of the Sarbanes–Oxley Act and the Lehman Brothers collapse gave birth to the Dodd–Frank Act, both thumping great tomes of new regulation that have caused many companies to complain that the medicine is far worse than the disease. The politicians believe they are responding to public opinion; the public was certainly outraged by the shenanigans at Enron and, at the time, believed that something should be done about it. And the only thing politicians can do about it is introduce new laws. So, surfing the wave of public opinion, new legislation comes into effect. The problem is that public opinion is fickle, fluid and ephemeral. The public changes its mind, but once they are on the statute books, regulations last forever.

The link between democracy and government regulation as illustrated in the World Economic Forum survey is explained by this mechanism, although we should slightly qualify it by noting the role of the media. A key factor is how effective is the press in amplifying the *vox populi*. An angry public, fanned by a free press, makes politicians pass new laws. So it might be better to draw a causal link between the freedom of the press and the burden of government regulation. After all, Singapore is a democracy and has the lightest touch in terms of the regulatory burden placed on companies but ranks 150th in surveys measuring freedom of the press,[38] below Zimbabwe and Burma. That is not to say that a free press is a bad thing; merely that the downside of a free press seems to be an increased regulatory burden.

Scylla and Charybdis

In Homer's epic poem *Odyssey*, the hero, Odysseus, is trying to get home from Troy to his wife in Ithaca. On the voyage he has to sail his ship between Scylla and Charybdis, between the rock and the whirlpool. This combination is deadly for mariners and is, according to tradition, sited in the Strait of Messina that separates Italy from Sicily. On one side is the high, unyielding rocky cliff of Scylla; on the other side, less than a bowshot away, is the watery fury of the whirlpool: a spinning, chaotic maelstrom that can absorb whole ships. The dilemma for Odysseus is that in steering away from one hazard, he must confront the other. In the end, he decides to sail close to Scylla and potentially lose only a few sailors on the rocks rather than risk losing his whole ship in the whirlpool.

Scylla and Charybdis became idiomatic, in both the classical world and post-Enlightenment Europe, of being faced with a difficult choice between two evils. The popularity of the metaphor springs from its

Manichaean coupling of opposites: one is hard, the other permeable; one is immobile, the other in constant motion; one is land, the other sea.

This metaphor is still apt in the twenty-first century. It vividly describes the challenges facing a CEO steering the company through dangerous seas. On the one side, Scylla represents government regulation: a looming cliff of unyielding legislation that needs careful navigation so as to avoid crashing against its rocks and hidden reefs. On the other side, Charybdis is the whirlpool of social media: fickle, shifting and often contradictory; it has the inchoate power to destroy corporate brands in an instant. In *Aesop's Fables*, there is an interesting variant of the myth in which Charybdis is actually the creator of the opposing rocks. In one mighty gulp, the whirlpool sucks away so much water that the mountainous cliffs rear up and become visible for the first time. In a similar way, it is the whirlpool of public opinion that has created the forbidding ramparts of government regulation.

It is the interplay between these two obstacles that makes them so dangerous. On their own, it would be fairly easy to just sail around either of them but the two are closely coupled, and that coupling is getting ever closer. In most of the case studies that we look at throughout this book, the CEO faces two main challenges when dealing with a corporate crisis, namely, how to deal with the regulator and how to deal with the media; in other words, dealing with the 'court of law', on the one hand, and the 'court of public opinion', on the other. So to manage a corporate crisis is to sail your ship smoothly between Scylla and Charybdis. We will spend the rest of this chapter looking at the interplay between the two.

Cupidity and stupidity

I went to a Muse concert in a huge stadium in London recently. Muse is a rock band renowned for its spectacular live shows and so much part of the mainstream that it performed at both the opening *and* closing ceremonies of the London Olympics. The band's music is a fusion of many styles; bombastic power chords, hammering bass lines, crunching guitar solos interspersed with delicate moments of emotional frailty. It fits somewhere in the continuum between Queen and Radiohead.

Halfway through the set, the whole stage is suddenly transformed into a giant Reuters dealing screen with 20-foot-high share prices flashing across from left to right. A portly man in a pinstripe suit parades across the stage and then prances down the catwalk, way out into the middle audience, showering money left and right while the band pounds out its anti-banker anthem 'Animals'. The song urges the banker to kill himself and 'do us all a favour'.

The crowd screams its derision. A startling chiaroscuric light show beams its searchlights up to the heavens. Arms are pumping the air at a 45-degree angle. The mob chants its hatred of evil financiers. And I can't help thinking this: whichever hell Joseph Goebbels currently inhabits, he must be smiling right now. This is a twenty-first century Nuremberg rally.

All organisational departments have been affected by the shifts in public opinion and regulation, but some industries have had it worse than others. And none has had it worse than the banking sector. Much of the recent criticism of banks is unfair and hypocritical. When the public blames banks for 'irresponsible lending', that is like blaming your spouse for making you fat by allowing you to eat too many chocolates. Surely the responsibility lies with the consumer? After all, no one puts a gun to your head to force you to take out a mortgage.

Unfair or not, the result has been public opprobrium towards bankers, and governments, swift to pick up on the public mood, are imposing increasingly onerous regulatory burdens on this benighted industry.

According to a survey by Thomson Reuters, regulators around the world announced 14,215 different changes to financial services regulations in 2011. That comes after 12,179 regulatory changes in 2010. That means on every single day, there are 60 new rules being introduced to govern the conduct of banks throughout the world. No wonder the fastest-growing department in every bank is the compliance department. For example, in 2012, having been hit by large regulatory fines, JPMorgan added an extra 4,000 compliance staff to its payroll. One wonders how any commercial enterprise could cope with the sheer volume of all this red tape.

The worst part of it is that most of this red tape is completely pointless. The financial crash of 2008, whose after-effects still rumble on today, shouldn't be seen as a sign that things were broken but rather that things were working properly. Finance is cyclical. There are booms and then there are busts; always have been, always will be. So a crash is not abnormal but normal. It is the natural, self-imposed corrective to exuberance. The crash is the sign that things are being put to rights again, that the market is taking care of itself.

The legislator's fantasy that regulation will create a perfectly tranquil market, bubble-free, unperturbed and featureless is not just a pipe dream but a dangerous fallacy. A good illustration is the story of the Chartered Financial Analyst (CFA) Institute, founded in 1947. The idea was to set up a self-regulating body, similar to those in accounting and legal services, which would turn market participants into 'chartered professionals'. By the mid 1980s anyone who wanted a lucrative job in investment banking was encouraged to pass their CFA exams. This involved an onerous three-year course covering all aspects of financial analysis, including valuation methodologies, economic theory, corporate finance, derivatives and portfolio management. At least a quarter of the course was devoted to ethical issues and client conflicts of interest. In addition, by the mid 1980s every major market exchange around the world had its own regulator, which set out standards of practice on issues such as insider trading, market integrity and the primacy of client interests. Each of these exchanges required market professionals to pass their own unique set of exams in order to participate.

All these regulatory regimes were well in place by 1986 when financial services were deregulated and globally integrated capital markets began to emerge. You might have expected, with such a core of chartered professionals, well trained in correct valuation methods and ethical standards, that markets would progress in an orderly, disciplined and smoothly expansive fashion. Instead, we got a tumultuous roller-coaster of scandals and market blowouts, including the Black Monday crash (1987), the Milken junk bond scandal (1988), the Savings and Loan crisis (1989), the bursting of the Japanese equity bubble (1990), the Asian markets crisis (1997), the Russian financial crisis (1998), the dot.com bubble (2000), the Enron crisis (2001), the global financial crisis (2008) and the Flash Crash (2010). The response to each successive crisis has been more regulation, such as the Global Settlement of 2003 and the Sarbanes–Oxley and Dodd–Frank Acts.

None of this is new. The whole cycle of boom followed by bust and then subsequent regulation can be seen as far back as the South Sea Bubble in 1720. This legendary incident is often seen through the spyglass of history as a monstrous scam deliberately designed to defraud the public; however, this view can be challenged. An alternative argument can be made that it was set up with the best intentions, was not a complete financial disaster and, in fact, ultimately fulfilled its purpose.

The South Sea Company was set up in 1711 in imitation of the successful East India Company founded a century earlier, in 1600. Much as the latter held a monopoly on trade with India, the South Sea Company was granted a monopoly on trade in slaves and other goods with Spain's colonies in Latin America. It is entirely plausible that the company could have shaken loose some colonies or trading posts from Spanish control just as the East India Company had with Portuguese entrepôts on the Malabar Coast.

In 1719 James Cragg, the Postmaster General and a major shareholder in the company, proposed a scheme to Parliament that involved a debt for equity swap: government debt would be swapped for South Sea Company shares. This was an elegant bit of financial engineering in which everyone emerged better off, at least in theory. The government, whose debt was bloated by the recent Spanish wars, was able to borrow money at a reduced interest rate and had much lower administration costs because it was replacing a multitude of individual bondholders with a single creditor: the South Sea Company. The company's shareholders benefitted because a reliable stream of income from government-backed bonds now underpinned their rather speculative investment. On paper, this is a classic win–win deal in which both sides gain from the transaction.

To put this situation in a current context, imagine an internet start-up approaching the government and taking over half the national debt. If you think such a proposal could only exist in fantasyland alongside unicorns, elves and one-eyed ogres, then cast your mind back to 2000. Similar deals were actually struck at the height of the dot.com boom; the astonishing takeover of Hong Kong Telecom by PCCW and the AOL/Time Warner deal are good examples of a minnow implausibly swallowing a whale. In the end, as with the South Sea Company, both of these deals ended in disaster; hubris leads ineluctably to nemesis.

In the case of the South Sea Company, although the debt-to-equity swap was a sound transaction, it was the subsequent events in the market that caused the scandal. In order to ease the passage of the deal through Parliament, prominent politicians were bribed with shares and so had a vested interest in talking the company up. These shares were effectively assigned 'on margin'; the recipient did not have to pay to own them and would just collect any increase in the share price as their 'profit' when handing them back. Most of the British establishment ended up as shareholders, including such luminaries as Sir Isaac Newton, Alexander Pope, King George I's mistress and three-quarters of both the House of Lords and the House of Commons. With the Great and the Good all extolling the company's worth, the price rose tenfold in a matter of months, from £100 to a peak of £1,000 per share in the summer of 1720. The bust followed just as swiftly and by the end of the year the price had fallen to £100 again.

In the course of this roller-coaster ride, the amount of money made was identical to the amount of money lost. That is the fundamental reality of markets: for every buyer there is a seller and vice versa. However, two important points can be made. The first is that, for most people, these were just paper profits and losses and, in any case, the shares were often bought 'on margin'. Second, those who made money kept very quiet but those who lost money were in uproar. From this, we can deduce the key maxim that links Scylla to Charybdis: history is written by the winners, but regulation is written by the losers.

In some ways, this is a reformulation of Edmund Burke's belief that 'All that is necessary for the triumph of evil is that good men do nothing'. In our formulation, the winners are silent because they don't want to draw attention to themselves and the losers complain vociferously. As a result, new regulations are introduced to pacify the losers. In short, the squeaky wheel gets the grease. This asymmetry in the responses of winners and losers is one of the engines that has driven the increasing regulation. Again, this may be a good thing (like a free press) because wrongs are being righted, but the downside is a huge increase in red tape.

The public uproar that followed the bursting of the South Sea Bubble was out of all proportion to the actual damage inflicted because most losses were only on paper. A careful examination of the financial records of the time does not show a huge increase in bankruptcies nor a wave of noble names forced to sell ancestral homes. But the Charybdis of public opinion is a vortex that distorts the truth behind facts. In the mind of the public, the incident was a morality play with the stock array of stereotypical characters: greedy bankers, corrupt politicians, trusty servants defrauded out of their hard-won savings and destitute widows thrown out of their homes and into the street.

The public outcry required a regulatory response, which was duly delivered in the form of the Sir John Barnard's Act 1734. This Act banned the practice of shortselling (selling stock that you do not own) and remained on the statute books until it was finally repealed in 1860. In a striking example of how history repeats itself, the Financial Services

Act 2010 (introduced in response to the 2008 crash) also attempted to restrict shortselling. This is just one of the many attempts in the 300 years since the South Sea Bubble to tame the markets through regulation. We note in passing the New York Act 1792 to prevent stock jobbing, the German Exchange Act 1896 to prevent futures trading and the Hughes Commission set up after the Panic of 1907.

All of these regulatory interventions were introduced in response to public outcry after a market crash and attempted to restrain the natural ebb and flow of markets. But, as with King Canute and the waves, they were just as ineffective. Shortselling, stock jobbing and futures trading are all conduits through which investors can express their views on the appropriate price of stocks. Shutting down those conduits thus makes the market less rather than more efficient. It is as misguided as trying to improve communication by cutting people's telephone lines.

To conclude, the finance sector is a perfect microcosm in which to demonstrate the workings of Scylla and Charybdis. The market booms. The market busts. The public vents its anger. The politicians respond by introducing legislation to demonstrate that they're 'doing something about it'. The legislation is misguided, which creates new market distortions and the whole cycle begins again. Standing on the sidelines, all you can do is note the wry irony of a legislator who responds to the free expression of opinion in the public arena by quashing the expression of opinions in the market arena.

As a footnote, and to complete the story, the South Sea Company continued well into the nineteenth century. Along the way, it was the cause of the memorably named 'War of Jenkins' Ear' (1739–1748) between Britain and Spain. It eventually entered the lucrative whaling industry, the oil industry of its day, creating the historical precedent for the Falklands War between Argentina and Britain in 1982. In the end, despite its turbulent history, the South Sea Company paid its investors all that they were owed and more, so maybe it deserves a better reputation than that which posterity currently grants it.

The fickle court of public opinion

Regulation is a government's attempt to right a publicly perceived wrong. One reason why it is so often flawed is the fundamental instability at the heart of all liberal democracies. Whenever there are plenty of different things to choose from and the freedom to choose whatever you want, sooner or later you'll end up with an unequal distribution of those goods throughout the populace. The functioning of the market inevitably creates winners and losers. Diversity of goods plus freedom of choice thus creates inequality: the greater the freedom, the greater the inequality.

That reality is the contradiction at the heart of all liberal democracies: the freer they are, the more unequal they are. The more people are free to choose, the less likely that we can all be equal. However, to counteract that, there is also a strong, human, emotionally driven impulse to share things equally inside the group. It is a basic instinct of co-operative group behaviour. This dynamic coupling of a market-driven push to inequality and a societal pull towards egalitarianism is the dynamo that drives regulation in liberal democracies.

In April 2013 YouGov conducted a poll that asked respondents, 'which of the following is the most unacceptable?'. The results are given below in brackets:

- A company paying £10 million less tax a year using legal tax avoidance methods (44%)
- A rich individual saving £1 million a year using legal methods (41%)
- An individual saving £10,000 a year by lying (37%)
- Those not in poverty lying to get an extra £40 a week in benefits (26%)
- Those in poverty lying to get £80 a week in benefits (11%)
- A worker doing work for cash to avoid paying tax (6%)

The first observation is that the acceptability of the actions has little correlation with whether or not the law is actually being broken. In fact, quite the opposite. A company avoiding tax legally (44%) is perceived as far worse than a sole trader avoiding tax illegally (6%). Likewise, it seems that a rich individual can do no right (41%) while a poor one can do no wrong (11%), regardless of the law. If there is any rhyme or reason to the results, then it seems to be driven by scale in a classic cataxic hierarchy. Scale is working here in two ways: the amount of money concerned and the size or scale of the protagonist. So a company is bad where an individual is good, and an action involving £10 million is worse than an action involving only £80. In effect, the further away is the action from the daily life of Joe Public, the more heinous it is.

Here, then, is the crux of the problem. Regulation is a reasoned and rational edifice; Scylla is a cliff of logic. But new regulation is driven by the court of public opinion; Charybdis is a vortex of individual human emotions.

A good way of illustrating this situation is to look at how the role of the regulator has changed. The Thatcherite revolution of the 1980s kicked off a wave of public utility privatisations. However, since these were often monopolistic entities, some new mechanism was required to introduce market forces into the arena. This was done by setting up a new market regulator for each industry: Ofwat for the water sector, Ofgem for gas and electricity, ORR for the railways and the FCA (or the SEC in the US) for banking and finance. The role of the regulator was to promote competition and the orderly functioning of the markets. Though the playing field was sometimes tilted in favour of new entrants, the regulator's main focus was economic and its tools were price controls and other market mechanisms. The aim was to ensure that the benefits of increased competition flowed through to the consumer in the form of better service and cheaper prices. However, this mission has gradually become corrupted as the regulators have become instruments of government policy rather than impartial economic overseers.

'To a man with a hammer, everything looks like a nail.' This terse aphorism is used by pragmatists to torment idealists. We all know people who are so wedded to a particular ideology that they think they have the universal solution to everything; that everything is a nail to their hammer. But this dictum has a mirror image: 'When a nail is sticking out, every tool is a hammer.' It is this second adage that explains why the role of the market regulator has become corrupted. When a government is trying to change public perception, then every tool available will be used to achieve that end, regardless of what that tool was designed for. This is the equivalent of hammering in a nail with a pair of pliers.

A good example is provided by the Energy Companies Obligation introduced by the government at the beginning of 2013 and enforced by Ofgem. A fivefold increase in oil prices over the last decade means that energy costs have soared and, in that rising market, so have energy companies' profits. Such a scenario is a gift to the populist press. The story almost writes itself: pensioners freeze to death because they cannot afford to heat their homes while fat cat energy bosses award themselves record bonuses. It reads like something out of Dickens and provokes a similar wave of public outrage. Something *must* be done!

But what *can* be done? The cause of the problem is rising oil prices driven by a global market and as such is beyond government control. But what tools are to hand that are inside government control? The answer is the energy regulator Ofgem. This is the pair of pliers that can hammer in the nail. The solution is to force the energy companies to pay for the installation of energy-efficient boilers in the houses of the poor. This has a double benefit. It helps the UK meet its national carbon emission targets and provides affordable warmth to the needy. No more public outcry about impoverished pensioners freezing to death.

It is an elegant solution but the downside is that the role of the regulator has been compromised. Ofgem is no longer an impartial market facilitator but instead an instrument of government policy. As pointed out earlier, free markets result in the unequal distribution of wealth. So, in a sense, a regulator tasked with creating an efficient market is being tasked to promote inequality. To then ask the regulator to correct moral inequalities resulting from market forces is to turn its original mission statement on its head. It's like asking Greenpeace to start a wholesale trade in whale meat.

This energy sector illustration is just one example of the phenomenon. In the financial sector, the Anti-Money Laundering (AML) and Know Your Client (KYC) regulations introduced by the FSA are a similar example. These rules, which are now commonplace throughout the developed world, force banks to check the backgrounds of their customers. You can no longer just turn up at a bank with a suitcase full of cash and make a deposit. The bank will want to know where that money came from and that you really are who you say you are.

On the surface, the logic of the argument is quite straightforward:

1. Crime is bad.
2. Criminals use the financial system.
3. If you restrict criminals' access to the financial system, you will reduce crime.

From the government's perspective, of course, there is a fourth unspoken benefit:

4. Forcing people to disclose sources of income increases your tax take.

AML and KYC regulation places an intolerable burden on the financial sector, particularly on smaller companies, and fuels a huge increase in administrative costs. But alongside this increase in red tape is the transfer of moral responsibility, which is potentially far more serious. If you're a small fund management firm, it is now your responsibility to police the system on behalf of the government or you risk going to jail. You thought you were in the money management business but you've been deputised into the law enforcement business. Good luck!

As with the case of the energy companies, the public desire for 'something to be done' results in the government introducing regulation that transfers both the moral and fiscal burdens onto the corporate sector. The government can demonstrate that it has responded to the wishes of the electorate at no extra cost to the taxpayer. So, on paper, everyone appears a winner ... apart from the corporate sector, which ends up carrying the can in the form of more red tape.

Rolling back the red tape

In almost every election, hopeful candidates promise to deal with the problem of excess red tape. These challengers, who are competing against incumbents, must distance themselves from the status quo. So their message is one of change; a new broom to clean out the sclerotic bureaucracy and failed policies of the 'out of touch' existing political establishment. Sadly, once elected, this almost never happens. Think of Obama's slogan: 'Change we can believe in.' Two years later, as president, he was humiliated in the House of Representatives elections by the Republican Tea Party clamouring for change and smaller government.

A study of Western democracies in the last 50 years shows a steady, inexorable increase in the volume of legislation. In 1985, Parliament passed some 6,000 pages of legislation. By 1995 it was 11,000 pages a year and, in 2010, the figure reached 16,000 pages. Likewise in the US, in the 1970s Congress passed 2,000 pages of statutes every year. In 2010 this figure had reached 8,000 pages a year, a fourfold increase. In November 2012, Speaker of the House John Boehner refused to put the Senate's Immigration Bill to the vote because it was 1,300 pages long and no one had actually been able to read the whole thing. In Europe, the legislation required for a country to join the EU now runs to 200,000 pages. If the whole thing was printed out and bound into volumes, it would make a line of books that would cover ten dining tables in a row. Who could possibly ever read it all?

The law of unintended consequences means that the momentum of legislation will always increase. However, every now and again there are some small chinks of light; signs that a backlash against excessive rules can succeed. The most optimistic example is the work of the late Hans Monderman (1945–2008), a Dutch civil engineer. In 1982 he was made head of the road safety team in Friesland in the north of the Netherlands. In an attempt to reduce injuries and fatalities resulting from road accidents, he came up with a radical new solution: removing all the traffic signs, speed bumps and chicanes. His theory was that, if you relied on the driver's common sense and intelligence instead of road markings and barriers, you'd get better results. He was fond of proving his theory in an alarming way, walking backwards into traffic at busy intersections that he had redesigned. As he expected, the traffic always stopped for him.

By removing traffic signs and blurring the distinction between the pedestrians' pavement and the vehicles' carriageway, he was removing responsibility from the state and returning it to the individual. The best news was that it actually worked. In the absence of state-imposed restrictions, a new civic interchange developed between pedestrians and drivers based on mutual respect, which resulted in fewer accidents and traffic delays. This is a good example of how rules are sometimes not required. It is a clear rebuttal to those who fear that taking away regulations will result in chaos, anarchy and rampant selfishness. Monderman's traffic systems show that people are perfectly capable of organising themselves without the need for externally imposed regulations.

During the last decade, Monderman's ideas have influenced urban planners around the world. If you visit the Victoria & Albert Museum or the Science Museum in London, you'll walk down Exhibition Road, which has been re-zoned in line with Monderman's design principles. There is no longer a distinction between pavement and road. The two have been fused together into a single surface with a large-scale diamond pattern. The result has been a drop in accidents and slower traffic.

However, this has come at quite a price. It took 18 years, £29 million, a court case and endless consultations to achieve the redesign of 400 metres of road. An Olympian could run down it in just 43 seconds. Whether this should be held up as an example of victory over red tape or a defeat remains unclear.

Maybe a clearer example of the benefits of rolling back red tape is provided by trade treaties, which reduce restrictive practices and promote economic growth. This was the guiding principle behind the establishment of the Single European Market. The EU sought to guarantee four freedoms: the free movement of capital, goods, services and people. Between 1986 and 1992, 12 different sets of national regulations were replaced by one common European law. This law has created major benefits, such as reduced complexity of regulations and thus cost to companies marketing products in the European Union.

One transformative element of the common EU law was the 'mutual recognition' principle. Member States agreed to grant equal validity to each other's laws and technical standards. Thus a product that was certified for sale in France by French bureaucrats was automatically certified for sale in every other EU country. This has led to regulatory arbitrage, which has had a positive impact on reducing red tape. Companies seek certification for their products in the country with the least onerous bureaucratic burden, which has the effect of promoting lighter-touch regulation and increasing bureaucratic efficiency.

The Single European Market is still a work in progress, particularly on the services side, but it has been successful in boosting trade. Since its introduction, trade between EU Member States has risen from €800 billion in 1993 to €2,800 billion in 2011 and the single market now covers over 500 million consumers in 27 different countries. It may thus come as a surprise to some that the EU can be held up as a poster boy for actually *reducing* red tape.

At a global level, the General Agreement on Tariffs and Trade

(GATT) and subsequently the World Trade Organization (WTO) scored some spectacular successes early in the post-war period. For example, in 1950 the Torquay round of negotiations lasted eight months but resulted in 38 countries making 8,700 tariff concessions, which, on average, reduced tariffs on global trade by 25 per cent. As time went by, more countries joined the club but the negotiations became more sclerotic as a result. The Uruguay round, which started in 1986 with 123 participating countries, took seven years to reach final agreement on reducing tariffs in areas such as textiles and agricultural subsidies. This was followed by the Doha round, which started in 2001 with 159 participating countries, and is yet to reach a final agreement.

The credibility of the WTO has suffered as a result. Now that so many different countries are voicing their opinions, it may prove impossible to come to any meaningful accord. So attention is now shifting to bilateral deals whereby substantial progress can be made in reducing barriers to trade by limiting the number of countries at the negotiating table. In 2013 the EU and the USA began negotiating a Transatlantic Free Trade Agreement (TAFTA), which would weld the two continents of North America and Europe into a single free trade zone containing a billion consumers and representing two-thirds of the world's GDP. If it's successful, the benefits accruing to Western economies as a result of reducing red tape in sectors such as pharmaceuticals, agriculture and financial services could provide a substantial stimulus to growth. At the same time, the USA is also negotiating a Trans-Pacific Partnership (TPP), which would unite the Asia Pacific region in a similar way. The TPP is being negotiated by Pacific Rim countries: Australia, Brunei, Chile, Canada, Japan, Malaysia, Mexico, New Zealand, Peru, Singapore, the USA and Vietnam. If the TPP and TAFTA go ahead, the USA will be at the centre of a global free trade arena that, deliberately or not, has left two enormous countries out in the cold: India and China. These are the two elephants that are *not* in the room.

The riddle of Charybdis

These new initiatives in freeing up world trade and removing excessive bureaucracy from commerce are redolent with possibility. Trade talks are notoriously slow and unproductive, but there is a good chance that the cynics will be confounded and some major positive benefits will be achieved. Having the majority of the world's economy operating under a single common set of rules would clearly be better for trade than the current thicket of diverse national regulations. At the same time, even if it is just a single set of rules, there are still likely to be a lot of them. The bigger question, then, is why should government regulators become involved in deciding what can or cannot be sold to consumers in the first place? The principle of 'caveat emptor' or 'buyer beware' is perfectly good and has stood the test of time. Would it not make more sense to return the burden of responsibility to the consumer? Why not let them accept the consequences of their own choices? Just like Hans Monderman's traffic experiments, can't we just rely on the common sense of the person in the street?

There is a curious contradiction at the heart of modern consumerism that could be called the 'Riddle of Charybdis': if the individual has been given so much power why do they not also have responsibility? Logically speaking, if the customer is king, they should also take responsibility for their own choices; that is, caveat emptor. But in the modern world, the regulator has assumed responsibility. It is the regulator who decides what can be sold and what is banned from the marketplace. Markets have self-regulating properties; someone who sells rotten vegetables will end up with very few customers. Markets thus tend to sort themselves out under a caveat emptor regime, without the oversight of a regulator. It's often said that nowadays kids are forced to grow up too quickly; that adolescence is curtailed; that they're treated as little adults before they're ready. The riddle of Charybdis suggests that the opposite is also true: adults are treated like kids. One definition of an adult is a person who takes responsibility for their own actions. In wielding power without accepting responsibility, consumers appear more adolescent than adult.

How did this happen? When did consumer rights become more important than consumer responsibilities? Part of the reason for the shift has been the gradual depersonalisation of the shopping experience. When the friendly local butcher is replaced by a large, anodyne supermarket chain, shopping transactions lose their human face. You're no longer being 'sold' something by a trusted local community member, you're collecting items from shelves in a place that looks similar to a cavernous warehouse. Another potential reason is that the market has been *too* successful in delivering choice. When faced with 45 different mobile phones, all of which do pretty much the same thing, the breadth of choice can induce feelings of anxiety. What if you make the wrong choice? What if you want to change your mind later? This soon leads to the question 'what are my rights?'

So depersonalisation and the bewilderment of choice have led the regulator to assume responsibility and become a champion for consumer rights. The regulators have stepped in and decided what can and cannot be sold. But in trying to harmonise and rationalise everything, they may, in fact, have made things more risky rather than less so. A good example of this situation is financial services regulation. A financial services regulator decides what financial products are appropriate to sell to the general public and which are too 'high risk' for the person in the street. In making this decision, it is introducing a new type of risk, channelling a tidal wave of consumer funds into a particular product. This lemming-like behaviour inevitably causes market distortions. In addition, risk evaluation is an inexact science, which is often accurate only after the fact. The CDO crisis, examined in Chapter 2, is one such example.

Regulation assumes that the area in question can actually *be* regulated. Unfortunately, this implicit assumption behind attempts to regulate is often just not true. The law of unintended consequences means that introducing regulation produces outcomes that are sometimes the opposite of what was intended. Regulation can be compared to a plaster cast. When a fracture occurs, the plaster cast can take the weight of the limb while it has time to repair. But once the cast exists, the body comes to rely on it, with the result that the muscles become weaker rather than stronger. Likewise, the more regulation is introduced to define consumer rights, the less responsibility the consumer is willing to accept and the greater the potential liability for any company selling in that market. 'Buyer beware' becomes 'seller beware'.* Plaster casts, of course, are intended as only a temporary measure. Regulation, on the other hand, seems permanent.

Twitter: the voice of adolescence

The whirlpool of public opinion goes all the way back to the Roman *vox populi*, the vociferous mob of common people that could only be appeased with gladiatorial spectacles in the Circus Maximus. But Charybdis has been updated in the last decade with the invention of Twitter. This social microblogging service is the quintessence of irresponsibility and power and so is maybe less the voice of the people and more the voice of adolescence.

Messages on Twitter (tweets) must be only 140 characters long. Some see this constraint as an artistic enabler. It's true that self-imposed straightjackets sometimes produce a higher art form, such as poetry over prose or black and white over colour film. In a similar vein, Twitter enthusiasts uphold the length-constrained tweet as a modern haiku; a perfectly composed thought; an elegant concision of truth; a distillation of the immaculate. Sadly, the vast volume of traffic on Twitter falls far short of this ideal. Poetry, according to Wordsworth, is 'emotion recollected in tranquillity'. Most tweets are big on the emotion but fall short on the tranquillity. To surf through the messages on

---

* The principle of caveat emptor has not completely disappeared; rather, it has been driven underground in a figurative sense. It now resides in all the disclaimers and small print that consumers never bother to read at the bottom of the contract.

Twitter is to ride a wave of ill-directed sentiment. A whole constellation of maladjusted youth is tweeting about how they feel right now to whoever wants to listen. Twitter traffic is instinctive, more sudden reflex than sober reflection, massing together to make a whole, churning vortex of adolescent angst. There is so much of it, a million tweets every minute, each one clamouring for attention, that the only way to stand out is to do one of two things: be funny or express extreme (offensive) views. If you want to go viral, you might do both; if you do neither, you're unlikely to get an audience. This is not a communication channel for measured judgements or considered debate. This is Charybdis and in this emotional whirlpool, public opinion is formed and new trends born.

If you can't beat them, join them

When the public expresses an opinion, the corporate world must listen. Twitter has transformed the way marketing is done because it provides real-time feedback on how advertising messages are received. Previously, if you wanted to find out what people thought you'd commission an expensive market research survey to answer that question. But Twitter provides an ocean of instantaneous public opinion, expressed and logged for free. By observing the response to your ads in the 'Twitterverse', you can gauge the impact that your message has on the general public.

The Economist described how Nestlé monitored Twitter during the US Super Bowl to see how the ads of its competitors were being received by viewers.[39] Nestlé has a Digital Acceleration Team whose job is to evaluate how the company's products are faring against competitors in social media networks. In February 2013 team members were gathered at the company's Lake Geneva headquarters on Super Bowl Sunday to watch the Baltimore Ravens play the San Francisco 49ers. In fact, they were not watching the game but a different screen displaying a digital map showing the 'buzz' in the social media landscape in real time. Suddenly, the game was blacked out as a faulty relay device in the stadium triggered a power cut. For the next 34 minutes there was nothing to see, just players milling about aimlessly in the semi-darkness waiting for the lights to come back on. That half-hour was a seminal moment for ad executives; the established model of marketing was turned on its head and the advertising world was irrevocably changed.

Super Bowl advertising slots are notoriously expensive. Over 100 million viewers watch the game each year and this huge audience commands a premium price. A 30-second advertising slot costs $3 million. It's expensive, but it offers a chance to talk to almost the whole of America in one sitting so is considered worth it. The Super Bowl blackout changed all that. Into the void stepped a number of opportunistic companies posting humorous tweets composed on the spur of the moment. Audi, which was pushing a new car with LED headlights, tweeted 'Sending some LEDs to the @MBUSA Superdome right now'. Tide, the detergent makers, tweeted 'We can't get your #blackout but we can get your stains out'. The best offering was that of Oreo cookies: 'Power out? No Problem. You can still dunk in the dark.' This message was retweeted 16,000 times and garnered 20,000 'likes' on Facebook.

Here's the moral of this story: the advertisers who gained most from the Super Bowl opportunity weren't those who had paid millions for an ad slot but those who were the most agile and responsive.

Marketing used to be all about promoting a single message on a global level. What's more, that message was broadcast and so it was going only one way. Ads used to interrupt TV programmes and were seen as a necessary evil to be endured in exchange for free TV shows. Now ads want to be found, 'liked' and shared. The Twitter revolution has turned advertising into a two-way conversation. Disgruntled tweets can emerge from anywhere around the world. Youngsters filled with attitude can trash brands and comparison-shop from the comfort of their own sofas. Companies need to monitor the Twittersphere and deal with negative publicity promptly via social media channels.

A change in mindset is needed. Responding to complaints on

Twitter is a chance for organisations to show a human face. *Forbes Magazine* described how Bank of America got it badly wrong when responding to customer complaints relating to mortgage foreclosures. It tweeted: 'We would be happy to review your account with you to discuss any concerns. Please let us know if you need assistance.'[40]

The response from the public was along the lines of 'you can help by not stealing people's houses'. Even worse, the company sent the same message to every customer. If it wanted to show its human, caring side, it failed completely. Bank of America succeeded only in 'reinforcing [its] image [as] a faceless, heartless conglomerate'.

In conclusion, to deal with the rock and the whirlpool, with Scylla and Charybdis, follow the old maxim 'if you can't beat them, join them'. One effective way of dealing with the enormous wave of new regulation is to be involved in the framing of that regulation in the first place. This accounts for the huge growth in political lobbying over the last 40 years that we discussed at the beginning of this chapter. Its influence over the political establishment is reinforced by the 'revolving door' effect whereby politicians, on leaving office, are hired by lobbying firms. Since 1998, of the 198 members of Congress who left government to return to the private sector, 43 per cent became lobbyists, paid by corporations to influence the very people they were previously working alongside. Likewise, when Charybdis makes its voice heard via Twitter, the best response is to co-opt the same channel and tweet right back. Just try to be a bit more skilful at it than Bank of America.

In this chapter we've treated the government regulator and the court of public opinion as two separate entities but there are times when these two forces are merged together into a single institution. Such a body fuses the moral indignation of an angry public with the quasi-governmental apparatus of a public sector entity. The result of this amalgamation is the non-governmental organisation (NGO). The threats posed to multinationals by NGOs deserve a chapter all to themselves.

CHAPTER 6

NGOs and organisational activism

> The nine most terrifying words in the English language are: 'I'm from the government and I'm here to help.'
> *Ronald Reagan*

SUBSTITUTE NON-GOVERNMENTAL ORGANISATION FOR GOVERNMENT AND many executives would be tempted to say that Reagan was right on the money. NGO activism has exploded in recent years, encompassing historic institutions such as the United Nations and the Red Cross, cottage industry protest movements and global organisations like the World Wide Fund for Nature and Amnesty International.

Because it covers so many different types of organisation, the term NGO itself is hard to define. Anyone and anybody can set themselves up as an NGO. For discussion purposes, focusing on a given organisation's 'orientation', that is, what it wants to achieve – improving human rights, protection of the environment and so on – and 'scale', local, regional, national or international, is the usual approach to describing an NGO. And there are more of them each year. The number of NGOs currently operating in the US alone is estimated at 1.5 million. Russia has a mere 450,000 while India, with 2 million NGOs in 2009, has just over one NGO per 600 Indians, which is proportionally more than the number of schools and health centres in the whole country.

And NGOs have certainly kept the acronym writers busy:

BINGO – Business-friendly International NGO or Big International NGO
TANGO – Technical Assistance NGO
TSO – Third-sector Organisation
GONGO – Government-operated NGO (set up to resemble NGOs in order to qualify for outside aid or to promote the interests of government)
DONGO – Donor-organised NGO
MANGO – Market Advocacy NGO
PANGO – Party NGO, set up by political parties and disguised as NGOs to serve their political agenda

Edmund Dene Morel, a lowly Liverpool shipping clerk, is credited with setting up one of the first NGOs. He did so at the turn of the twentieth century in opposition to one of the major corporations of the day, the King of Belgium. King Leopold, having decided that 'il faut à la Belgique une colonie' (Belgium should have a colony), took it upon himself to invade the recently 'discovered' Congo, not for Belgium, not for the state, but as his own personal fiefdom. Showing a shrewd grasp of Victorian PR, he persuaded the press that he was acting from humanitarian motives. In 1884 the *Daily Telegraph* opined: 'Leopold II has knit adventurers, traders and missionaries of many races into one band of men under the most illustrious of modern travellers to carry to the interior of Africa new ideas of law, order, humanity and protection of the native.'

But Morel saw a different story. From his office at Elder Dempster, the Liverpool shipping firm, he noticed that, although a lot of rubber and ivory was being shipped *out* of the Belgian Congo, the only things being shipped *in* were guns and ammunition. What, he asked, were the natives getting out of this arrangement? He began to investigate and quickly concluded that Leopold's well-publicised philanthropy was in fact 'legalised robbery enforced by violence'. But even Morel was unprepared for the barbarous levels of violence employed by Leopold's men; the routine penalty for a native failing to deliver enough rubber was the severing of his hand or that of his wife or child. A Baptist missionary wrote to *The Times*: 'The hands – the hands of men, women and children – were placed in rows before the commissary who counted them.'

In 1901 Morel quit his job and founded the Congo Reform Association. He set up a newspaper and enlisted support from luminaries such as Joseph Conrad (whose novel *The Heart of Darkness* was based in the Congo), Sir Arthur Conan Doyle and Mark Twain. He engaged with Christian missionaries who supplied him with eyewitness accounts and photographs of atrocities, and attracted patrons; the confectionery millionaire William Cadbury was one of his main financial backers. All strategies common to protest movements today.

And Morel's approach worked. Faced with growing international outrage, in 1908 the Belgian government finally acted, annexing the Congo from Leopold and bringing it under state control. The *Encyclopaedia Britannica* suggests that up to 30 million people may have died during Leopold's reign. Morel continued to campaign on behalf of the Congolese until 1913 when the Congo Reform Association folded.

To this day, the Congo Reform Association, its crusading drive and moral certainty, exemplify what most people still think of as an NGO – a humane, non-self-interested and trustworthy organisation, dedicated to doing good.

GONGOs and PANGOs are far from the only NGOs whose practices raise concern. In 1996 Al Gore wanted to prohibit an American NGO that had declared itself to be in 'opposition to the government' from receiving foreign donations. The NGO in question was Louis Farrakhan's Nation of Islam and the generous benefactor was Libya's then-leader, Colonel Mu'ammar al-Gaddafi. The Muslim group Hizb ut-Tahrir is banned in Germany and Britain despite its claims to be a peaceful socio-political movement. Amnesty International was criticised for its support of Guantanamo prisoner and Taliban supporter

Moazzam Begg, and Comic Relief UK was recently found to have invested publicly donated funds into arms and tobacco.

But when you encounter a cardinal point of risk wearing a halo, it's best approached with caution. Start with Rule 1: Don't deny anything before you are in full possession of the facts – and that includes facts about the opposition too.

How not to do it: *McDonald's v Steel & Morris* or 'the McLibel case'

In 1997, staunch vegetarians Helen Steel and David Morris were among a group of environmentalists distributing a pamphlet entitled 'What's wrong with McDonald's: Everything they don't want you to know' in front of a number of McDonald's outlets. Among the pamphlet's allegations were that McDonald's:

- Was complicit in causing starvation in the developing world
- Sourced from greedy rulers and elites and practised economic imperialism
- Wasted vast quantities of grain and water
- Destroyed the rainforests
- Sold unhealthy and addictive fast food
- Altered its food using chemicals
- Exploited children via its advertising
- Was responsible for the torture and murder of animals
- Poisoned customers with contaminated meat
- Exploited its workers and banned unions
- Hid its malfeasance.

When news of this pamphlet reached McDonald's, the company immediately filed a lawsuit against Helen Steel and David Morris – respectively, a gardener and a London postman – for libel. And with a robust tradition of both suing and winning libel actions, having taken out cases against more than 50 organisations, including Channel 4, it must have thought its work was done.

This time was different. Steel and Morris refused to settle. Lacking money for legal fees, and denied legal aid, they decided to represent themselves. This alone should have set the alarm bells ringing, but McDonald's kept going, and set against the burger giant's team of top libel lawyers, the David-and-Goliath nature of the case meant that instead of the story being quietly squashed, it quickly caught the public eye. Newspaper columnist Auberon Waugh described it at the time as 'the best free entertainment in London'.[41]

Perhaps realising that things weren't working out quite as it had hoped, McDonald's tried to settle the case in June 1995 by offering to donate a large sum of money to a charity of Steel and Morris' choice on the condition that they stopped criticising McDonalds in public even if they continued doing so in private. Steel and Morris said they would agree to the conditions if McDonald's stopped all of its advertising and only referred the chain via its friends. Steel and Morris even recorded the conversation, which was later leaked and further damaged McDonald's reputation.

And so the show ran and ran. The case lasted more than ten years and went down in history as the longest-running of its kind in England. Thousands of articles in the word's press, including front-page coverage in the *Wall Street Journal*, plus international TV and radio coverage in the USA, Canada, Australia, New Zealand, Ireland, France, South Africa, Belgium, Netherlands, Germany, Japan, Trinidad, Russia, Spain, Italy, Switzerland, Austria, Thailand and Israel, served to draw more attention to the leaflet's contents than could ever have been achieved by hand.

In a victory that was barely Pyrrhic, two subsequent hearings found *some* of the leaflet's claims to be libellous and others to be true; McDonald's was responsible for exploiting children via its advertising, paying its workers relatively low wages, remaining antipathetic to unionisation and treating animals cruelly. The judge awarded £60,000 damages to be paid by Steel and Morris, which paled next to the estimated £10 million McDonald's had spent on legal fees (and which Steel and Morris still refuse to pay) but nothing could make up for what some media commentators called the biggest corporate PR disaster in history. Or the longest-running negative ad in the world.

What McDonald's failed to take into account was that Steel and Morris weren't journalists or broadcasters such as Channel 4, and thus wary of the legal whip, they were activists. Like whistleblowers, activists tend to be strong-willed people, reluctant to give in to pressure and sometimes even actively spoiling for a fight. If McDonald's had taken even a cursory glance at the McLibel 2 (as they came to be known) it would have seen that their leaflet was no real threat and, almost as importantly, that they had nothing to lose and were merely seeking publicity. What better than a long, drawn-out court case?

The McLibel 2 should have come under 'known knowns' rather than a bolt out of the blue. Just as businesses can identify their customer base, so they should also be aware of what sort of NGO attention they may attract and prepare accordingly. Because when a company's customer base sides with the NGOs, they're in for real trouble.

NIKE: learning to work with and listen to NGOs

> My daughter said she wanted some Nike trainers. I told her, 'you're twelve, make some'.
>
> *Jeremy Hardy, comedian*

Nike was publicly shamed as a result of its labour practices. Adverse publicity badly tarnished the company's image and hurt sales. Change became a matter of survival.

In 1991 an NGO labour activist, Jeff Ballinger, exposed the appallingly low wages and horrendous working conditions of factory workers in Indonesia. In the following year, Ballinger published another exposé of Nike in *Harper's Magazine* highlighting how Nike subcontractors were paying workers as little as 14 cents an hour. A wave of mainstream media attention followed, as did public outrage.

The timing was perfect for the NGOs. Spearheaded by a new generation of computer-savvy under-thirties, grass-roots activists and NGOs worked with PR practitioners to subvert Nike's PR campaigns ('Just Don't') for a fraction of the corporate budget. Their message was shared at a speed and breadth that advertisers could only dream of.

In a response best described as tardy, in 1996 Nike established a department tasked with 'improving the lives of factory labourers'. It wasn't external, it didn't involve NGOs and it didn't achieve its goal, which was to silence the opposition. Then, in 1997, in response to reports about terrible working conditions in Vietnam, a Nike spokeswoman was quoted as saying 'What is Nike's responsibility? These are not our factories.'

As with whistleblowers and rogue employees, the credibility gap between the values and lifestyle the company promoted and the evidence of its behaviour grew too vast for mere advertising to close. Nike's efforts at promotion turned into further opportunities for public outrage. As the company began expanding its 'Niketown' stores across the USA and Europe, it saw a barrage of organised and sometimes violent protest. The sports media even began challenging people like Michael Jordan about their endorsement of Nike products.

American college students in particular began making their feelings known. People throughout the world started burning Nike shoes instead of wearing them and by 1998 the company's earnings had plummeted by 69 per cent. *Not* wearing Nike had become the new cool.

The belated realisation that ignoring supply chain responsibilities was bad for business and that the company's global reputation – a key source of competitive advantage – was at stake, caused Nike founder and chairman Phil Knight to finally declare in May 1998, in a speech to the National Press Club, that 'the Nike product has become synonymous with slave wages, forced overtime, and arbitrary abuse'. He added, 'I truly believe the American consumer doesn't want to buy products made under abusive conditions.'

Nike finally started dealing with the brutally exploitative culture of its working practices abroad. Fighting fire with fire, in 1999 it created the Fair Labor Association, a non-profit organisation (a BINGO), to work with human rights and labour representatives at the local level, and to establish independent monitoring and codes of conduct, including a minimum working age and a maximum 60-hour working week.

And having muffed Rules 1 and 2, Nike weighed in with Rule 3: hiring an outside firm, Ernst & Young, to audit working conditions at its plants abroad. In an effort to change the culture, it developed a code of conduct for employees and managers, issued on pocket-sized cards in the local language, and provided extensive training programmes for the managers of its contracted factories. It cut off ties with some of its factories in Indonesia and put its Vietnamese factories under review.

During 2002 to 2004 Nike performed over 600 factory audits, including repeat visits to problematic factories. It aggressively greened its supply chain, reducing and ultimately eliminating the use of toxic chemicals from its production processes. NGO activists acknowledged that the monitoring at least dealt with some of the worst problems, such as locked factory doors and the use of unsafe chemicals, but continued to apply pressure.

Abandoning its former strategy of denial, Nike introduced a new policy of transparency, which led to it publishing a complete list of the factories it had contracts with abroad and a detailed 108-page report revealing conditions and pay in its factories. Even more importantly, it acknowledged that widespread issues still existed in its south Asian factories. In June 2007 Nike said its corporate social responsibility (CSR) campaign was no longer just 'a risk and reputation management tool' but a core 'business objective' and that, from then on, its growth strategies would build on the four pillars of sustainability, brand enhancement, capital efficiency and profitability.

More recently, Nike has positioned itself at the forefront of other social issues – notably those that have nothing to do with it but which reflect well on its core brand image – such as child obesity. For a mere $50 million (small beans to a billion-dollar company), it was first to support Michelle Obama's Lets Move! initiative and collaborated with the US Departments of Health and Human Services and Education to 'educate and inspire kids to pursue outdoor activities'.

It took a long time, a great deal of discussion and even more negotiation, but eventually Nike regained its credibility. Its sustainability efforts began to be trusted and even endorsed by governments and, almost as importantly, celebrities. Indeed, by differentiating itself from competitors who fail to adopt these initiatives and practices, Nike has managed to reposition itself as one of the good guys and gone from a position of rapid decline to being one of the strongest sustainable global brands. Nike has regained its cool.

Nothing's secret any more: animal welfare

In October 2012, Mercy For Animals (MFA), a non-profit animal advocacy organisation based in Chicago and aiming to '[end] the exploitation and abuse of animals', secretly videoed workers at a Butterball factory farm (Hybrid Turkeys) mistreating turkeys. An MFA activist had joined the workforce and, working undercover for three weeks, documented workers dragging birds by their wings, violently slamming them into tiny transport crates, and showed birds with serious injuries and illnesses including rotting eyes, broken bones and open wounds covered with flies. The footage was then shown on national TV.

When the story broke, Butterball stated, in keeping with the executive script for rogue companies, that it was 'shocked' by the undercover video and operated a 'zero tolerance policy for any mistreatment of [its] birds'. The company then condemned the 'former associates', that is, workers – who were quickly fired – and announced that, as a result of an internal investigation, it was evaluating its animal welfare policies. Officials at the farm where the footage was filmed described the behaviour of its employees as 'isolated'.

Butterball, which accounts for 20 per cent of all turkey production in the USA, repeatedly insisted that it trained its employees to be humane and had an array of fine welfare policies; the public, however, remained unconvinced. Exculpatory sound bites did nothing to remove the image of birds with open wounds covered with flies in the weeks leading up to Thanksgiving.

Matt Rice, MFA's Director of Investigations, laid the blame fairly and squarely at the feet of the top brass:

> These abuses are a direct result of Butterball's complete lack of animal welfare policies, training, or oversight. ... Butterball expects a few untrained workers to move thousands of crippled turkeys into transport trucks, and pays workers by the load, not the hour.[42]

Eventually, David Libertini, Hybrid Turkey's managing director, having again claimed the company had 'zero tolerance for animal abuse', hired an outside investigator to review the company's welfare and training practices. Helen Wojcinski, Hybrid Turkey's new science and sustainability manager, promised to instal video cameras to monitor the euthanising of its turkeys and to assign a vet to review the tapes (possibly one of the least fun jobs in the world).

But Mercy For Animals executive director, Nathan Runkle, remains unconvinced. 'Unfortunately, every time we send in an investigator they emerge with shocking evidence of animal abuse,' he told ABC. And as recently as 2013 yet more video evidence was produced by MFA revealing abuses at Hybrid Turkey's farms in Canada that were nearly identical to those discovered at their farms in the USA.

The cost to Butterball's reputation was considerable, and the battle for customers' hearts and minds is ongoing. Its significance, as far as organisations and animal welfare are concerned – much like working conditions for overseas workers – is that nothing is secret anymore. Few activists are as proactive and determined as animal rights activists, and their list of corporate scalps is growing. McDonald's and Target felt compelled to fire their egg producer after *60 Minutes* aired footage of its hatchery hens in deplorable conditions – footage captured by MFA activists and then handed to the network – a contract worth millions of dollars to the egg producer.

NGOs such as the Humane Society have taken a more conciliatory approach and managed to persuade food outlets, including Burger King, Costco Wholesale, Denny's and Wendy's, to buy at least *some* of their eggs from producers that allow hens to roam. Elsewhere, however, animal rights activists are stepping up the pace. SHAC – Stop Huntingdon Animal Cruelty – an international animal rights campaign to close Huntingdon Life Sciences (HLS) in Cambridge, Europe's largest animal-testing laboratory, has supplemented the releasing of videos online with the alleged firebombing of houses owned by HLS executives, clients and investors. In 2009 and 2010, 13 members of SHAC were jailed for between 15 months and 11 years on charges of conspiracy to blackmail or harm HLS and its suppliers. The Southern Poverty Law Center, which monitors US domestic extremism, even described SHAC's operations as 'frankly terroristic tactics similar to those of anti-abortion extremists'. In 2005 an FBI counter-terrorism division official referred to SHAC's activities in the USA as domestic terrorist threats.

Animal rights activists are relentless and cameras are cheap. Like the McLibel 2, they are immune to threats and inspired by a cause and thus believe they are morally right. The best way for organisations to deal with these types of NGO is to not provide them with footage in the first place. However, in the face of negative publicity, should it occur, an organisation's response must be swift, transparent and believable.

David and Goliath – when David is wrong

The *Brent Spar* was a North Sea oil storage and tanker loading buoy operated by Shell (then the Royal Dutch/Shell Group of Companies). With the completion of a pipeline to Sullom Voe in Shetland, it was no longer needed and Shell and the government negotiated disposal options for over three years. The preferred solution was to tow the rig to deep water 240 km west of Scotland, break it up with explosives and sink it, along with the residual oil, sludge and waste remaining in its tanks. When, in 1995, the government announced its support for Shell's proposals, environmentalists were outraged and Shell had a crisis on its hands.

Using traditional direct action, Greenpeace activists boarded the *Brent Spar* in 1995 and occupied the installation for nearly a month, enduring water-cannon bombardment and attracting attention and garnering support, especially in northern European countries – notably Germany and the Netherlands – as well as opposition parties in Britain. In Germany, an unprecedented consumer boycott of Shell led to a 20 per cent drop in sales, personnel being physically attacked and a service station firebombed.

The ferocity of the public and political opposition caught Shell completely off-guard. At the time, it had no corporate website, no PR strategy and no means of putting its own case. And even when it did, nobody listened. When Greenpeace made the alarming claim that the *Brent Spar* was to be sunk with 5,500 tonnes of oil and waste on board – a claim that Shell vigorously denied – the figure was nevertheless picked up and used by the media and politicians at will. When, long after Shell had abandoned its plans to dispose of the *Brent Spar* at sea, the final figure was found to be some 10 tonnes of waste, Greenpeace issued an apology – really a half apology – as it said it continued 'in principle' to oppose dumping waste in the world's oceans.

But it was too late for Shell. Greenpeace's supposed moral superiority had blinded the media and its flawed science had been used without scrutiny. Film footage of the occupation of the *Brent Spar* and the subsequent water-cannoning made sensational TV coverage but at the price of scientific objectivity. In 1995, at the Edinburgh International Television Festival, media executives belatedly acknowledged this failure.

Greenpeace's reputation also suffered when it was forced to admit that it had been wrong. Like Morel and the Congo Reform Association, it had discovered that by targeting big brands and using new media channels, issues could be catapulted onto the international stage like never before. And not only Greenpeace learnt this lesson.

Andrew Vickers, now Shell's Vice President Policy and External Relations but then a press officer, said the decision not to sink the *Brent Spar* was 'a tipping point'. 'For Shell, it was about more than *Brent Spar*. Overplaying the legal card, underestimating the power of modern media tools and not seeing the deeper agenda are challenges that we work hard to address.'[43] In 1998, with the crisis long since passed, Shell announced its new 'best practicable environmental option', which was to reuse the *Brent Spar* as part of the base of a new ferry quay at Mekjarvik in Norway, which is where it now rests.

The *Brent Spar* episode brought home to Shell that brand and reputation are now global concerns and, as such, vulnerable to co-ordinated attack from international groups. And the bigger organisations are, the more likely the attacks. Heinz Rothermund, a managing director at Shell, said at the time: '*Spar* is not, as so many believe, an environmental problem. Rather it will go down in history as a symbol of industry's inability to engage with the outside world.'

But engage they must.

Golden rice: North versus South

In 2013 in an open letter to the respected US journal *Science*, 11 leading academics, including two Nobel laureates and the president emeritus of the US National Academy of Sciences, blamed Western NGOs

– including Greenpeace and Friends of the Earth – for stirring up opposition to GM technology. The scientific cause célèbre they were referring to was golden rice.

Vitamin A is essential for healthy skin and eyes and the immune system; its deficiency is almost unknown in the West, with its ample supplies of eggs, milk and cheese. In the developing world, however, Vitamin A deficiency is common and can lead to blindness, illness and death. Between 140 and 250 million children under the age of five are thought to be affected; indeed, over 670,000 children die each year and another 350,000 go blind.

Golden rice, developed with charitable funding from the Rockefeller Foundation, was designed to address this situation. Biotech company Syngenta managed to insert the Vitamin A gene from carrots into rice, and had even handed *all* financial interests over to a non-profit organisation, so there would be no resistance – it assumed – to the lifesaving technology from GM opponents. Animal testing had found no health risks and by 2002, except for the regulatory approval process, golden rice was ready to start saving lives and preventing blindness.

Only it hasn't. Because of opposition to the technology.

Greenpeace, with its blanket opposition to all GM crops, including golden rice, claimed that GM crops are prone to 'unexpected effects' and that using them to solve malnutrition was a risky distraction away from the real solution, which is to end poverty. Public unease at interfering with nature and political vacillation has left golden rice in a regulatory limbo.

In the meantime, while poverty remains unsolved, two agricultural economists, one from the Technical University of Munich, the other from the University of California, Berkeley, published an article in the journal *Environment and Development Economics* estimating that the delayed application of golden rice in India alone had cost 1,424,000 life years since 2002 ('life years' was used over 'lives' to account not only for those who died, but also for the blindness and other disabilities that Vitamin A deficiency causes). Even Greenpeace founder Patrick

Moore supports golden rice and has accused the NGO of crimes against humanity.

The public needs groups like Greenpeace and other NGOs to hold big companies to account when they put profits before health, as they all too often do. However, when that's not the case, the issue for organisations is how to deal with groups that seem motivated, not by science, but how they feel about the science, and how to put their case to a public preconditioned to believe one side is more inherently truthful than the other.

Working with NGOs – the truth is they're out there

In the last 15 years, NGOs working with business has been a growing trend, the impetus coming from both sides. The decline in the role of the nation-state and an increasingly globalised international economy mean that NGOs, especially those involved with the developing world, are increasingly drawn to where decisions are *really* being made – inside large organisations.

Maybe NGOs' motives aren't always straightforward. A recent article in *The Economist*[44] asks why, in the face of overfishing by local fishermen in the River Clyde in Scotland, did NGOs and pressure groups not intervene, targeting each individual responsible? The Firth of Clyde, to the south-west of Glasgow, is one of the largest and deepest areas of coastal water in the British Isles and sustained a thriving fishing industry for centuries. However, in the 1960s new technology in the form of sonar fish-location equipment, diesel engines and heavy trawl mesh tilted the odds heavily in favour of the fishermen and catches increased dramatically. But 20 years of overfishing has caused a crash in fish stocks and the Clyde is now an ecological desert almost devoid of marine life.

In 'one of Britain's biggest environmental disasters of recent times', the vocal environmental lobby was nowhere to be found – arguably because it is easier to target big business, regularly viewed as the bad guy by the public and governments: 'The Clyde's remote fisher folk – the hardy, easily romanticised agents of the Firth's devastation – are a less attractive target for greens than energy firms. They are also a constituency local politicians do not wish to annoy.'

It might be argued that NGOs go after big companies because they're an easy target, and so are likely to offer a cash payment to settle quickly. One might ask, are they really morally pure? Or do they target large firms for 'protection' money? Greenpeace are rumoured to make more money from corporate 'greenwash' consulting than from donations from the public. In counterbalance, organisations have realised that working with NGOs can be good for the bottom line. The public increasingly doesn't want to buy clothes made under inhuman conditions, eat food that has been tortured or support companies that damage the environment.

In the light of the credibility gap created by organisations' self-promoting environmental and social claims, the UN Environment Programme (UNEP) states that 'active dialogue and stakeholder partnerships assume unprecedented importance'. If Western retailers of products made in the developing world are to have access to credible information to reassure consumers, organisations need outside help. In other words, NGOs are useful because 'You can't clear your own name; only other people can do that for you' (Rule 5). Through working with NGOs, companies such as Nike have managed to draw attention to their environmental/worker policies and market themselves as good guys in areas that were previously the preserve of niche/green retailers.

McDonald's, once the NGOs' favourite bogey man, reacted promptly when Greenpeace revealed satellite maps showing significant new deforestation in the Brazilian rainforest caused by farmers cutting down trees to grow soy. Greenpeace's investigators searched records to see which companies were buying the rainforest soy and discovered one of them was McDonald's, which fed the soy to chickens destined to become McNuggets. 'We listened to what Greenpeace was saying about soy from the rainforest, and I think we surprised them at first by saying, "You're right. We have a problem here,"' said Bob Langert, McDonald's vice president for corporate citizenship.[45] McDonald's bought the soy from Cargill – the huge multinational company – which, when faced with an unhappy client, ultimately brought together other Brazilian soy traders and agreed on a deforestation moratorium. 'We have an active campaign to save the rainforests, and it turned out that we and McDonald's had very similar goals,' stated John Sauven, head of Greenpeace's rainforest initiative. 'We didn't start out with the idea of focusing on McDonald's or partnering with them, and someday we may well go after them again on other issues. But on this one, they played a highly positive role.'

In relation to sustainable development, NGOs have a wealth of expertise. The US Forest Stewardship Council (FSC), a non-profit organisation that promotes responsible management of the world's forests, offers forest stewardship certification (FSC) so that the end-consumer can be certain they are buying an environmentally sound product. And with increasingly complex supply chains, many corporations have benefited from the World Wide Fund for Nature's free advice.

And NGOs are connected. Sometimes this can be as much a blessing as a curse because companies that are serious about addressing particular issues can tap into existing NGO networks 'on the ground' in the countries where their suppliers operate. In reverse, international NGO networks can offer opportunities for poorer suppliers in the South to gain access to socially and environmentally 'progressive' markets in the richer North.

The other way around: NGOs working with business

In 2004 some 230,000 people died as a result of the tsunamis in the Indian Ocean and nearly 10 million were displaced. The media coverage was so graphic and horrifying that not only the general public and specific charities felt obliged to act. Companies with no prior interest in humanitarian relief felt compelled to help. The response, unfortunately, was slow, disorderly and frustrating for the United Nations and aid agencies. After the earthquake in Haiti, hundreds of well-meaning rescue workers travelled there and, in the absence of clean drinking water, food and medicine, promptly became victims themselves, adding to the recovery burden. The problem was logistics: how to get the aid to where it was most needed. Which, as it turned out, was a challenge faced by large organisations every day, if under less horrifying circumstances. So, how can organisations help?

United Parcel Service (UPS) has made its global fleet of aircraft, trucks and warehouses ready to supply emergency aid when needed. 'It's part of our corporate values,' says Eduardo Martinez, president of the UPS Foundation. 'You have to give back to the community – you have to be engaged in the community.'

And it helps if you're seen to do it.

UPS competitor Deutsche Post/DHL began humanitarian assistance in 2003 following the earthquake in Bam, Iran, in which 26,000 people died. As the world's largest air courier, its partnership with the UN, preparing airports to handle emergency supplies, proved enormously successful. 'We train our people on a regular basis so they're well-prepared for any situation,' says Susanne Meier, vice president of CSR Strategy at DHL. It now has three disaster response teams based at airports in Asia, Latin America and the Middle East. Each team has 80 experts and can deploy within 72 hours. 'We have a global footprint, we are a global company, so we want to do it on a global scale.'

Partnerships and supply chain management are the new buzzwords in the aid community. 'Ten years ago, logistics was not something that was on the agenda and on the map of the humanitarian – even being the backbone of the organisation,' says Brigitte Stalder-Olsen, director of logistics at the Red Cross. 'Today, it is on the agenda [of] the senior management team.'[46]

NGOs, like whistleblowers and rogue employees, should be

considered as part of an early warning system that something is badly wrong and a barometer of changing trends and consumer demands (for example, people don't want to be seen wearing clothes made by children). And because of the high – even if sometimes misplaced – levels of trust accorded to NGOs by the public, ignoring them is no longer an option. NGOs are public sector entities that reflect the strongly held opinions of individuals. As such, they can be seen as a fusion of elements from Scylla and Charybdis into a single body. Hence their power and importance; truly, the threat posed by NGOs must be taken seriously.

NGOs and organisations won't always get on. There is no middle ground between British American Tobacco and the health lobby. But when even fast-food companies such as McDonald's can sit down with Greenpeace, the way forward is clear. The reputational risks inherent in being on the wrong side of an argument with an NGO are high, and even higher now that a whole new front has been added to the field of battle in the last ten years: the internet. We touched on Twitter and other social media networks in the previous chapter, but it is now time to consider the other corporate risks that lurk out in cyberspace.

CHAPTER 7

The cyber threat

EVERY YEAR IT IS CUSTOMARY FOR THE US PRESIDENT TO PRESENT A STATE of the Union Address to Congress. This event is used to highlight national priorities, reflect on the condition of the nation and outline the forthcoming legislative agenda. In February 2013 President Obama chose to highlight the rapidly growing threat of cyber attack:

> We know hackers steal people's identities and infiltrate private e-mail. We know foreign countries and companies swipe our corporate secrets. Now our enemies are also seeking the ability to sabotage our power grid, our financial institutions, and our air traffic control systems. We cannot look back years from now and wonder why we did nothing in the face of real threats to our security and our economy.

Although he didn't specifically mention China, it was clear that's who he meant. Over the past decade, US officials have regularly and repeatedly accused China of carrying out cyber attacks. Those who remembered George W. Bush's hyperbole about the 'Axis of Evil' and the 'War on Terror' may have taken a cynical view of this warning. Was Obama attempting similar scaremongering but with a different pantomime villain in the frame? The most effective way to unite a nation behind you is to highlight a common national enemy. Was the cyber threat to which he referred as illusory as Iraq's weapons of mass destruction?

One week later, the cynics were quietened. Mandiant, a Virginia-based cyber security consultancy with close links to the US government, published its 'APT1' report. This was the smoking gun. The 80-page report spelt out in detail how Unit 61398 of the Chinese People's Liberation Army (PLA) had systematically stolen hundreds of terabytes of data from 141 Western companies in 20 different industries over a seven-year period. APT stands for 'Advanced Persistent Threat'. One of the surprises in the report was the length of time that the PLA, having established access to a corporate network, was able to milk it. The key point here is that such breaches can remained undetected for a long period of time. In the most extreme case, the PLA maintained access to a certain US multinational's network for almost five years, stealing data at will before the security breach was finally discovered. During that time, it stole information relating to a broad category of issues, including technology blueprints, manufacturing processes, test results, pricing documents, partnership agreements, business plans, emails and contact lists.

The method used by the PLA was fairly typical of all APT attacks and is worth summarising here. It starts with an email using a technique known as 'spear phishing'. Typically, this email will appear to be sent from someone inside the organisation, maybe a colleague or member of staff in the IT or HR department. The title will be innocuous such as 'Draft of press release' or 'Revised Employee Benefit Policy' and the text will encourage the reader to click on a link to open a document. Clicking on this link instals a malicious file (malware) on the victim's computer that creates a secret 'backdoor' which the attacker can exploit.

Most companies instal firewalls around their systems that prevent external viruses and malware communicating with their internal systems. In other words, their defences are focused on incoming attack. They're less efficient at detecting malicious traffic going the other way, from the inside out. An APT backdoor exploits this weakness. It initiates communication from inside the system to the attacker outside.

Having established this backdoor, the next step is to explore the system to understand how it is configured and to gather passwords and credentials of other users, such as system administrators, who may have better access privileges. Having gained privileged access as a result of this internal reconnaissance, the attacker is then able to move laterally around other related systems to identify sensitive databases, email servers and the best places to instal further backdoors. Once the system is thoroughly compromised, the attacker's malware can hide for months inside a network, gathering, archiving and encrypting useful files before sending them to the attacker outside.

Most APT attacks follow this sequence of steps. However, each occurrence is different because the malware used is specifically tailored to the victim's systems. Through examination of this malware it is often possible to work out who's behind the attacks. This is how Mandiant were able to connect the dots and point the finger at the Chinese government.

Pride comes before a fall

Mandiant faced a dilemma in exposing the PLA's techniques. In publishing the report, it carried out a public service by raising awareness of the cyber threat. It was very effective. In the months following the report's publication, Google searches for the term 'cyber security' soared to five times the previous level. The downside was that publishing China's attack methodologies meant they became effectively obsolete: once system vulnerabilities are known, they're far easier to block. The assumption must be that the PLA has already developed new, different and more complex attack methodologies that are currently invisible and will take much painstaking work to uncover. As with the predators and prey on the Serengeti plains, the battle between white hats and black hats in cyberspace is a constantly evolving struggle.

But the story doesn't end there. Having successfully denounced the Chinese (who continue to deny the charges), the USA for a brief moment held the moral high ground. So there was a certain hubristic inevitability about Edward Snowden's whistleblowing in relation to the cyber spying activities of the USA's own National Security Agency (NSA) a few months later.

Snowden had been working for the NSA in Hawaii via a subcontractor, Booz Allen Hamilton. Disturbed by the degree of surveillance NSA was carrying out on its own citizens, he began collecting a vast horde of incriminating top-secret documents. In June 2013 he decided to leak some of these documents to the *Guardian*. In an even more ironic twist, having declared that he 'did not want to live in a society that does these sort of things', he then fled from Hawaii to China (of all places!) before finally ending up seeking asylum in Moscow.

To date, only 1 per cent of Snowden's dossier has been published, giving details about the USA's cyber surveillance programmes and its telephone snooping on European heads of state, including Chancellor Merkel's mobile phone. It is rumoured that the material yet to be published is far more embarrassing. Public reaction to Snowden's revelations covers a broad spectrum of views. Some see him as the biggest and most damaging traitor in the history of the USA's intelligence services; others granted him awards and voted him 'Person of the Year' for 2103. However, one conclusion is incontestable: there is no moral high ground when it comes to spying in cyberspace. Every nation is doing it.

Introducing the cast of 'threat actors'

The plots of many classic thrillers and detective stories from the 1930s and 1940s revolve around dastardly foreign agents trying to steal formulas for poisonous gases, aircraft blueprints or nuclear technology. Alfred Hitchcock called these plot devices 'MacGuffins' – the objects that drive stories forward and after which heroes and villains chase. Think of the black statue in *The Maltese Falcon* and the Ark of the

Covenant in *Raiders of the Lost Ark*. The desired object is clearly of vital national importance, even though what it actually *is* remains obscure. Hitchcock believed that a MacGuffin's only relevance was as a catalyst for a good story; something around which could be wrapped some suspense and adventure.

It might be tempting to think of the cyber threat as a MacGuffin. A shadowy, ill-defined threat that makes a good story to sell to newspapers. The world of international spycraft and state secrets belongs in a James Bond film and seems far removed from the concrete realities of the corporate realm, unless you happen to be a defence contractor or operate a nuclear power station. Is a cyber attack just the latest in a long line of overblown threats allegedly facing organisations, like the Y2K bug or international terrorism – the current 'paranoia du jour'?

The evidence says no. Unlike terrorist attacks, which are few and far between, there are estimated to be around 120 successful cyber attacks every week against corporate targets in the USA alone. The threat is real and attacks are happening on a daily basis. An old stock market adage subverts Kipling's famous poem *If* and goes: 'If you can keep your head when all around are losing theirs ... you haven't heard the bad news yet.' Likewise, if you don't believe the threat of cyber attack is real you've probably already been attacked and just haven't detected it yet.

The examples given at the beginning of this chapter were focused either on the state or the individual: the Chinese government spying on the USA and the USA sifting through personal emails and phone messages to find evil doers within its own citizenry. Neither seem particularly targeted at the corporate realm. In addition, unlike in the early twentieth century, technology no longer belongs to a country; it belongs to a multinational. So intellectual property (IP), such as Coca-Cola's secret recipe or the designs for the new Apple iPhone, aren't 'state secrets' but corporate ones. What's more, Coke is bottled in China and the new iPhone is actually made there. The first people to know what a new iPhone actually looks like are the workers in a Chinese factory.

The key point is that it's a mistake to cast the cyber threat as a battle between nations. Rather, it should be framed as a modern extension of the age-old rivalry between large organisations. Cyber attacks should be filed in the same folder as traditional but immoral corporate practices such as theft, deception, market manipulation and guile.

Let's do a quick survey of the different malefactors in cyberspace; the 'threat actors' behind the different types of cyber attack. State-sponsored espionage clearly exists and always has, pre-dating the internet by hundreds of years. State-sponsored threat actors focus on critical national infrastructure, such as transport, energy and defence, seeking weaknesses or knowledge that could be exploited at a time of war. This is the only part of the cyber spectrum that could be described as a struggle between nations.

Though the Mandiant report fingered the PLA's cyber espionage as a government-sponsored activity, this categorisation is questionable. In the West, an 'army' is clearly an organ of the state, as far removed from commerce as it is possible to be. However, the PLA is actually one of the largest commercial entities in China, owning, either directly or indirectly, a vast portfolio of factories, real estate and other business concerns. In an economy in which political connections are the key to success, a retired general is a valuable business partner. This explains why the PLA has its fingers in so many pies in the commercial world. The PLA should thus be viewed as a business competitor as much as an organ of the state.

A second type of threat actor is the 'hacktivist'. Attacks by hacktivists tend to be ideologically driven. They're targeted at a particular company and aim to embarrass and defame the corporate brand. This is the cyber equivalent of protesters with placards outside corporate headquarters. In cyberspace, a common target for activists is the corporate website, which can be hacked to post anything from humorous parodies to malicious material. The other favoured target for hacktivists is documents or emails that prove links between a company and unsavoury business practice or partners. The aim of the hacktivist is to score a PR coup, such as newspaper headlines sullying the corporate brand. These coups tend to be one-off in nature, so this threat can be categorised as targeted but not necessarily persistent.

The third type of threat actor is persistent but not targeted: the nuisance actor. This is a purely opportunistic attack, similar to a passing thief stealing something from an unlocked car. The best example of a nuisance threat is spam. These unsolicited emails advertising dubious products or investment scams are a familiar irritation to all computer users. In 2011, an estimated 7 trillion spam messages were sent. The economic cost to internet users worldwide approaches $35 billion a year, reflecting the lost productivity of office workers and the additional equipment, manpower and software needed to combat the problem. The citizens of some countries seem to be particularly prominent spammers. A 2001 study by Cisco Systems measured the percentage of worldwide spam originating from different nations. India (14%), Russia (9%) and Vietnam (8%) topped the list. However, bear in mind that the person sending the spam message may not actually reside in the country it appears to come from. 'Botnets' are to blame – another common type of nuisance threat.

A botnet is a network of PCs that have been co-opted by malicious software and placed under the control of a master 'command and control' server. These PCs are effectively robotic slaves (bots) executing the commands of the master server. Because the PCs are scattered around the world, the physical location of the master server is effectively disguised. Thus, a spammer using a botnet can hide their identity because the spam appears to come from various random locations around the world. A good example is the Conficker botnet, set up in 2008, which now comprises over 10 million PCs sending out 10 billion spam emails per day.

From a corporate perspective, if several of the company's PCs become infected by a virus and turned into bots, your firm's assets have been hijacked and used for nefarious purposes. Spam is thus a nuisance threat in two ways: first, if you're actually receiving it and, second, if you're inadvertently sending it because some of your PCs have been co-opted into a botnet. Botnets are also used for distributed denial of service (DDoS) attacks. The aim of a DDoS attack is to make a corporate network crash by delivering so much incoming communications traffic from a botnet that it cannot cope. DDoS attacks are fairly common. A UK government survey found that 40 per cent of large companies in Britain had suffered some type of DDoS attack in 2012.

The threat of a DDoS attack is sometimes used to blackmail companies, just like an old-fashioned protection racket: pay me or else. The damage a DDoS attack could cause depends very much on the industry sector. Your corporate website being unavailable to customers for a few hours might just be a mild inconvenience. However, if you're Amazon, which makes $7 million profit per hour, a successful DDoS attack could be very expensive.

The fourth type of threat actor is a member of an organised crime network. The hacktivist is targeted but not persistent, the nuisance threat is persistent but not targeted but the organised criminal is both persistent and targeted. They know what they want and will keep trying until they get it. The chief motivation for organised crime in cyberspace is financial gain and the main target is credit card credentials. Identity theft is big business. A 2013 report by the Justice Department put the financial losses resulting from identity theft in the USA at $27 billion, which makes it the biggest form of crime by far. The total losses from the three next-largest categories – household burglary, car theft and stolen property – amount to only $14 billion. This is clear evidence that organised crime is now an online activity.

Organised crime networks have adapted an age-old form of extortion for the internet era; cyber ransom. A hacker penetrates the company's databases, selects an important file and then encrypts it. They then demand a relatively small amount of money to decrypt it. This is a lot cheaper than having to replicate or reproduce the data or invest in ultra-secure systems. How much would you pay to get a database of all your client records back? How much would it cost, in both money and time, to recreate it from scratch? Not surprisingly, many companies pay up and keep quiet about it.

The fifth type of threat actor is competitors. The modern business arena is a theatre of intense rivalry and any information your competitors can glean about your internal affairs is of value, sometimes game-changing value. This information can sometimes be gathered perfectly legally through scanning different sources on the internet. Online analysts often say that 90 per cent of everything that you might want to know about your competitors is freely available in cyberspace. All you need is the right type of search tool and some lateral thinking about where to look. You can examine photographs of your competitors' facilities on Google Earth, find PowerPoint presentations given at industry conferences in online archives or scan social media sources (Twitter, LinkedIn and Facebook) and personal blogs to find out where your rivals have been going and what they've been up to. Once you start looking, you'll be surprised by how much commercially sensitive information you can find perfectly legally on the internet. You can also assume your competitors are investigating you in the same way; a robust corporate social media policy is thus a good basic defence.

Searching and sifting of open sources on the internet is often called 'competitive intelligence' but it's only a short step across an often blurred line before it becomes industrial espionage. Even in the physical world, drawing this line is difficult. Imagine you're alone in a meeting room in your competitor's offices and you notice a commercially sensitive document that's been carelessly left behind on the table. You can do one of the following:

1. Read the front page but don't pick it up
2. Pick up and read the whole document
3. Pick up and photograph the whole document with your mobile phone
4. Put the document in your briefcase and take it away with you

From an ethical perspective, where should you draw the line? Most people would probably say 1 is fine and 4 is theft; the answer is thus somewhere between 2 and 3. But notice that the gradations are all based on your physical interaction with the document. In cyberspace, there is no physical interaction. Consider the following example. A hacker has successfully stolen a commercially sensitive document from a competitor and, keen to boast of their success, posts it to a hackers' chat room as evidence of their skills. One of your employees brings this situation to your attention. Do you:

1. Inform your competitor without reading the document?
2. Read the document on the site without downloading it?
3. Download the document and then inform your competitor?
4. Download the document but don't inform your competitor?

The ethical issues here revolve around whether or not the hackers' chat room is a public domain and whether you believe it's morally right to take advantage of your competitor's misfortunes. The answers depend to a great extent on the context: how intense is the commercial rivalry in your industry? How covert was the hackers' chat room? What is your corporate culture? From a legal standpoint, these types of issue in cyberspace are still very much a grey area.

Some activities, however, clearly cross the line. The PLA's activities, as described in the Mandiant report, comprise industrial espionage on a grand scale. An APT attack has taken time and effort to set up with the specific intention of stealing valuable information. This is criminal activity. If you don't believe that your competitors would go that far, then unfortunately history has some lessons to teach you. Many celebrated cases of industrial espionage exist, particularly in highly competitive industries. France's Groupe Bull allegedly stole secrets from IBM in the 1980s,[47] General Motors successfully sued Volkswagen for industrial espionage in the 1990s and Starwood Hotels accused Hilton of theft of corporate information on a grand scale in

2009. The most famous recent case involves Formula 1, in 2007, when McLaren stole technical data from Ferrari and then Renault stole similar data from McLaren.

None of the above cases involved a cyber-based attack, but they do illustrate that industrial espionage is not uncommon. In most of these examples, the main culprit was an employee who had moved to a competitor, taking a dossier of sensitive information with them. This breach of trust is as old as the hills but two important points are still worth making. First, as corporate databases become larger and more centralised and USB memory stick capacity increases exponentially, vulnerability to a rogue employee stealing data is growing dramatically. Second, the cyber threat appears in many forms. It mostly isn't cunning foreigners with advanced Trojan viruses; sometimes, it's as prosaic as an underpaid temp copying files onto a memory stick and walking out of the door with it.

Quantifying the cyber threat

Having described the different actors in the cyber threat arena, let's now put some figures on the scale and extent of cyber crime worldwide. The Ponemon Institute estimates that 122 successful cyber attacks on US companies occur every week and that most major firms suffer from a barrage of unsuccessful attacks on a daily, if not hourly, basis. A government survey in 2012 estimated that 93 per cent of large companies and 87 per cent of small companies experienced a cyber breach that year. In fact, most companies were breached far more than just once and most large companies more than a hundred times. A third of these breaches were caused by human error. The positive implication of this last fact is that improved policies and better implementation of procedures can dramatically enhance cyber security. The financial benefits are obvious when you consider that a cyber breach typically costs a large company £650,000.

Awareness of the cyber threat is also growing in the corporate world, as demonstrated by the rapidly expanding cyber security industry, now worth $100 billion per annum. Generally speaking, most companies now have fairly robust firewalls to protect them from incoming malware but are relatively weak at network monitoring and incident management. This leads to a second measure of cyber awareness: the median duration of APT attacker activity which is the length of time it typically takes to discover malicious hacker software hidden in the corporate network. In 2011 the median was 416 days but by 2012 this figure had dropped to 243 days. Most companies have now become much less complacent and are getting better at spotting APT attacks. However, 243 days is still far too long a period in which to give a potential competitor continuous online access to your corporate documents.

One interesting new development is a change in who discovers cyber breaches. In the past, two-thirds were discovered by law enforcement agencies, which then notified the corporate victims. However, recently almost a quarter of cyber breaches are being discovered after notification by a third party: suppliers, customers and even competitors. This development is a sign of the growing realisation that the cyber threat is a threat to the whole corporate community and that a community response is therefore warranted. Where previously a corporate victim of a cyber attack would keep quiet about it to avoid embarrassment or censure, it is more common these days to share the information in industry groups. Cyber attacks are so prevalent that there's nothing to be embarrassed about. In addition, sharing information about the latest hacker techniques and tactics with trusted third parties helps everyone to mount a vigilant defence. Now is the time for all good men...

The aerospace, defence and energy sectors are top of the list in terms of APT attacks. A third of all attacks are directed at these targets, as might be expected, because their intellectual property is of particular value to both competitors and foreign governments. Technology sectors such as IT and telecoms are also high on the list of favoured targets. Recently, there has been a growing focus on the professional services sector, such as lawyers, accountants, consultants and financial intermediaries. These types of firm are trusted third parties to their clients and therefore privy to much confidential information while being relatively soft targets. Finally, two different industries have both seen a fourfold increase in APT attacks over the last year: pharmaceuticals and media/entertainment. While at first glance these seem odd bedfellows, what they share in common is IP with huge commercial value. Drug formulas, clinical trial results and digital movies make tempting targets for cyber crime.

Understanding the principles of cyber defence

The cyber threat is often presented as an exotic new phenomenon, only comprehensible to technocrats and teenagers; however, the reality is more mundane. Cyber crime is crime, just with a new logo. Many of the principles of cyber defence have close parallels in the physical world. Indeed, frequently there's a physical dimension to a cyber attack; for example, in the surveillance phase in which the attacker is casing the joint, figuring out the physical range of your office Wi-Fi and the best place to sit so as to access it with a laptop. Alternatively, it could be in the attack phase, as the perpetrator gets past your front desk to plant a virus contained on a memory stick. In fact, it's best to think of cyberspace as just one more domain that an attacker may exploit in their attempt to steal data. The 'cyber' threat refers more to the target of the attack: information stored in electronic form. In order to steal it, an attacker will exploit many avenues, social and physical as well as technological.

Cyber crime does have one important distinction, however. It is the only type of crime in which something can be stolen from you while you still remain in full possession of it. This is because digital data can be endlessly copied with no diminution in quality. The copy, to all intents and purposes, is identical to the original. When digital data is stolen, it is actually being copied rather than removed, which is why it is sometimes so difficult to work out whether or not you've actually been attacked. In that sense, cyber crime is the *invisible* crime – not because it takes place out of sight in cyberspace but because the victim may never know that it has actually happened.

Protecting against cyber crime involves a number of psychological elements that make it antithetical to the typical CEO. In most cases, the latter is action-orientated, forward-looking and driven by results. Cyber security is the opposite of this. First, it is essentially defensive. There is little point in seeking out the identity of the attacker. They'll be shrouded behind many proxies and probably operating from a different country. Even if it were possible to definitively identify the perpetrator, the legal jurisdictions in cyberspace are fragmentary and incoherent. If you discover that a state-sponsored Iranian hacktivist is messing with your corporate network, there's not much you can do to retaliate. Your best strategy is a passive one: frustrating attackers through better defensive measures rather than actively pursuing the aggressor.

Second, cyber security is backward-looking. The main challenge lies in establishing whether or not you have, in fact, been successfully hacked. This involves combing through reams of historic network data and patiently analysing it for anomalies that might indicate a successful breach. Having spotted a suspected incident, it needs to be forensically examined, quarantined and patched, and new policies rolled out to close this loophole to future attackers.

Third, 'results' in cyber security are almost always negative. All users implicitly assume that the corporate network should work perfectly all the time and be completely secure. So if, at any time, the IT infrastructure falls short of this idealistic benchmark, the blame game begins. The success of the cyber security department is measured by the absence of negatives rather than the presence of positives. There is only downside since the starting assumption of 100 per cent perfection has eliminated the upside. In summary, an action-orientated, forward-looking, results-driven CEO may find that their head of cyber security not only speaks a different language (technobabble) but is also psychologically estranged from them.

A key dilemma for cyber security policy lies in finding the right balance between protecting the data and protecting the network. Though at first these things may seem to be one and the same, there are in fact two different strategies here, which can be crudely summarised as 'data citadel versus firewall'. If the main focus is on protecting sensitive information, a 'data citadel' strategy is appropriate. This involves setting up a highly secure location on the network, similar to a bank vault, in which to store these documents. The alternative approach is to focus on the security of the network as a whole, restricting an adversary's initial access to any part of the system. The physical analogy here is swipe cards in the office lobby or, perhaps, passport control at the airport.

Each approach has its strengths and weaknesses. Let's focus on the 'safe network' strategy first. Internal communication is increasingly critical in large organisations; the larger they become, the more important it is. It is often a key factor in determining corporate success or failure. Everyone with a commercial role would like fully transparent sharing of information to help win new business. For a salesperson, the ideal corporate network is one in which everyone inside is a trusted colleague and everyone outside is the enemy. In their view, borders and checkpoints should only exist at one place: the perimeter. Inside the boundaries, there should be a completely free flow of information. Their message to the IT department is 'guard the frontiers but otherwise keep out of my way'.

Most large organisational networks are a mishmash of different equipment, technology, software and user preferences. They've evolved over time, developing organically at different rates in different places and sometimes with large chunks suddenly bolted on as a result of corporate takeovers. In concept, they form a single common platform but, in practice, they're less a monocultural Midwestern wheat field and more a complex ecosystem like a tropical rainforest. Many of the 'species' in that rainforest are ill-documented and may even be unknown. To qualify that last statement, they may be known to the natives but unknown to rational scientists, who, in this case, are the cyber security team in head office. This means that the practical difficulties inherent in enforcing a 'safe network' strategy are immense.

Several technological trends are making the situation worse. The first is 'cloud computing', whereby documents and software are held not locally but in a public network (a cloud). This approach brings big economic benefits such as scalability, shared resources and reduced investment costs but the downside is that documents held in the cloud are outside corporate control and therefore potentially less secure. Cloud computing services are doubling in size every year so it would seem that the economic argument is currently outweighing security concerns in the corporate arena.

The second trend is the use of non-standard equipment in the workplace, a phenomenon known as 'bring your own technology' or BYOT for short. The pace of development in consumer hardware such as smartphones and tablets is so rapid that lumbering corporate IT departments struggle to keep up. Once the CEO has started to use their iPad to access the corporate network, it's hard to say no to anyone else in the company. The latest 'must have' consumer gadget will always be more desirable than its dull, dated corporate counterpart; Apple's rise and Microsoft's demise reflect this reality. The BYOT trend also results in cost advantages. If your employees are responsible for supplying their own laptops and mobile phones, the company clearly makes substantial cost savings. Again, however, a security cost is involved. If the devices accessing the corporate network are no longer under corporate control, the chance of a security breach is much higher. There is also the problem of hardware disposal. How many employees are meticulous enough to erase the hard drives on their personal laptop or iPhone when they sell it on eBay and upgrade to a new model?

The third issue is email, in particular the 'cc' and 'bcc' functions. The corporate environment is becoming increasingly collaborative.

Most companies encourage a team approach and the list of people who need to be kept in the loop seems to be growing all the time. The average number of recipients for a corporate email has more than doubled from 3.1 to 7.3 people over the last ten years. This situation increases risk in two ways. An email with a large number of recipients is a gift to a hacker who is trying to harvest email addresses and connect the dots in the corporate hierarchy. In addition, most people use mailing lists on their PCs to send out team emails. These mailing lists are probably out of date, which means that sensitive information is often sent to people who have left the company.

The final issue with a 'guard the frontiers' network strategy is the problem of where to draw the boundary line. This is more difficult than first appears. The obvious answer is that employees are inside the wall and everyone else is outside. But what about temporary employees? Or contractors? Or trusted third-party suppliers that are collaborating on the project? Or customers who are part of the pilot? The more you consider the problem, the more you realise that no crisp dividing line exists. It is more a zone of diminishing trust, a liminal space of confidence or a smooth transitional gradation from insiders to outsiders.

For all of the above reasons, the latest thinking in cyber security is moving away from erecting a barrier at the frontier. The notion of an electronic Hadrian's Wall to keep out the barbarians has conceptual flaws, as we've shown. The emphasis is shifting from keeping the network safe to keeping the data safe. This 'information security' approach recognises that it's impossible to protect everything, particularly when the volume of corporate data is both vast and highly dispersed. Following the military maxim that 'he who defends everywhere, defends nowhere', the best strategy is to put the really important stuff in a secure vault – like gold in a bank.

Sadly, this approach also has problems. First, by putting everything important in one place you're creating a target, sometimes an obvious one. A burglar, when entering a house, will head straight for the safe because that's where the valuable stuff is sure to be. It may require some initial reconnaissance beforehand, maybe a chat with the builder who installed it or an innocuous-seeming house visit, but once the location of the safe has been identified a burglar's job becomes much easier. Likewise, in the cyber world, network reconnaissance and traffic analysis will soon yield the location of the secure data vault or 'data citadel'. An APT attack takes time, patience and skill. A data citadel makes a worthwhile target for this investment of effort. The more secure the data citadel, the more likely that it contains data of value and therefore the more persistent and targeted the APT attack will become. Unlike a burglar who spends less than an hour in someone's house, the average APT attack lasts for eight months; plenty of time to crack the toughest vault.

The second issue with the data citadel approach is a problem of human nature. The more laborious the security procedures, the less likely they are to be followed. Imagine a reference document kept in a room behind seven locked doors. You need to check some of the details in that document fairly regularly. Fairly soon, the whole palaver of going through seven locked doors for a quick check of a single fact becomes too burdensome, particularly when you're working under time pressure. The temptation to make a copy of the document for your own personal use becomes too great. So you make a copy and keep it on your laptop, purely on a temporary basis, to improve your working efficiency. At that moment, you've just defeated the whole purpose of that secure data vault. This scenario demonstrates that the biggest challenge associated with a data citadel is not in building the thing but in ensuring that the sensitive data stays inside it; leading us to the third issue, which can be summarised as: Attack the stagecoach, not the bank vault.

Fans of cowboy films or heist capers will know that the best time to steal valuable things is when they're being transported. Think of the Great Train Robbery. The clue's in the title; it happened on a *train*. Banknotes were being transported from London to Glasgow and were far more vulnerable to theft while on the train than in the secure vaults at either end of the journey. Likewise, the key vulnerability of a data citadel is when the data is being sent in or out. Documents are interactive. Someone has to write them and other people download and read them. If malware can be introduced into an early draft of a document, this infected file will be deposited into the data vault and exploited by hackers later. In the physical world, the film *Ocean's Eleven* depicts just this situation. The 'grease man', played by Chinese acrobat Shaobo Qin, hides inside a trunk, which is then stored inside the bank vault. Later, he emerges from the trunk to open the vault from the inside and let the others in.

In summary, the 'safe network' and 'data citadel' approaches both contain flaws. The former because of the difficulties involved in establishing a secure frontier in an era of cloud computing, BYOT and collaborative third parties. The latter because a vault becomes a prime target for persistent attack and human error. The interactive nature of documents compounds these inherent vulnerabilities. The best strategy is to combine elements of both: patrol the borders and have a strong safe. Just remember that the attacker is likely to enter through the weakest part of your network, probably a poorly configured, small, overseas branch office; having carried out their reconnaissance, they'll then head straight for the data citadel.

One final attack strategy is worth mentioning – the 'waterhole' – whereby the initial target is well outside the corporate network. Hunters often build their hides near waterholes in the knowledge that, at dusk, most animals in the area will come there to drink. So, rather than pursuing their prey through the bush, they can sit and wait for their victims to come to them. Hackers use a similar strategy, but the waterhole in cyberspace becomes a website of mutual interest. Say, for example, the attacker is interested in aircraft engine technology. They'll target a public website that manufacturers of jet engines will visit regularly, for example a parts supplier's site or an industry news forum. If they successfully compromise this site, then all visitors to the site will also become compromised. They therefore gain maximum reward for minimal effort. Breaching that one single public site will net them a dozen other corporate victims, all involved in the attacker's industry of choice.

Legal jurisdiction in cyberspace

Having summarised the different defence strategies, it's worth briefly surveying the landscape of legal jurisdiction in cyberspace. Sadly, the view here isn't pretty; in fact, the picture is completely incoherent. All new frontiers start out as lawless regions, think of the Wild West and realise that cyberspace is no different. But there's an additional problem. Whatever regulation does exist is hard to enforce because of problems with territorial jurisdiction. Laws generally apply inside a country and cyberspace is not a country; it is beyond geography.

In the developed West, no common, overarching framework of cyber legislation exists; it is more a confusing patchwork of different statutes. For example, in the UK the Computer Misuse Act 1990 makes it an offence to deliberately penetrate, alter or damage computer systems without authorisation. The Data Protection Act 1998 also makes it an offence to knowingly or recklessly obtain or disclose personal data or procure the disclosure without consent from the data controller. One of the ironies of the latter is that it sometimes punishes the victim. In April 2011 Sony's PlayStation network was hacked and personal details from 77 million accounts stolen. In January 2013 the Information Commissioner's Office (the UK's data regulator) fined Sony £250,000 for a serious breach of the Data Protection Act, arguing that the hack could have been prevented if Sony had used more up-to-date software. This example is a clear reminder that cyber regulation cuts both ways.

Sometimes the legislation struggles to keep up with technological developments. A good example is provided by the Dutch court that ruled in 2011 that Wi-Fi hacking wasn't a crime. The Netherlands enacted a computer hacking law in the early 1990s whereby a computer is defined as a machine involved in the 'storage, processing and transmission of data'. A Wi-Fi router does not store data. As a result, the judge ruled that it was not a computer and therefore the computer hacking law wasn't applicable.

The EU has recognised that current legislation in Europe is fragmented and small scale. It is thus working on a cyber security directive that seeks to harmonise a minimum level of network and information security across the European Union. The proposals focus on government institutions and critical elements of national infrastructure, such as the energy, telecoms, health care, transport and financial sectors. If the proposals are passed, operators will be required to notify a new cyber security regulator of any security breaches they encounter. They also appear to be setting up a new mechanism for Europe-wide co-operation, which will enable EU Member States to share information about particular incidents and offer early risk warnings over a new secure network.

In the USA, the Cyber Intelligence Sharing and Protection Act (CISPA) was passed in the House of Representatives in April 2012 but failed to get through the Senate. CISPA was an attempt to update the 1947 National Security Act to include provisions for cyber crime. As its name suggests, the aim of the Act was to encourage the sharing of information gathered by the government's intelligence agencies with the private sector. However, the bill was robustly opposed by libertarian groups such as the Electronic Frontier Foundation and the American Civil Liberties Union, which believed that it undermined the right to privacy of internet users and would usher in an era of Big Brother-style government snooping. Their fears were somewhat justified when Edward Snowden revealed in the summer of the same year that the NSA was *already* doing so to a far greater extent than was previously understood.

CISPA has stalled, leaving an unsatisfactory lacuna in the corpus of cyber legislation in the USA. But if the situation in the developed world is not all that could be hoped for, the state of affairs in emerging economies is even worse. In China, hacking is illegal and carries a maximum penalty of a seven-year prison sentence. In practice, though, hacking is commonplace. Hacker conferences and training academies are openly advertised and public opinion is broadly tolerant of cyber crime; it's seen as somewhere between a national sport and a lucrative career path.

In other countries there is no legislation at all. In Brazil, computer hacking isn't a crime and the police have to prove that fraud has actually taken place in order to prosecute. It is no surprise therefore that Brazil is fast becoming one of the world's main centres for cyber crime. The Brazilian Federal Police have claimed that eight out of ten of the world's hackers are based in Brazil. This is either a deliberate exaggeration from a department looking for more funding or a perverse nationalistic boast, but it's certainly true that Brazilian-based cyber criminals are a serious global threat. The situation in Africa is scarcely better. Only three countries in Africa (South Africa, Botswana and Zambia) have legislation dealing with computer-related crime. In addition, 73 per cent of the continent's software consists of illegal, pirated copies, which are a common source of malware. Egypt is gaining a reputation as a source for cyber espionage malware, while Nigeria is world-famous for its fraudulent email scams.

How best to manage the risks

To conclude, most cyber defence strategies have conceptual flaws, the legal environment is fragmentary and incomplete, offering little protection to organisations, and the adversary is anonymous and hidden behind layers of proxies. What, then, is the best action to take? The answer lies in internal change.

The first step is to recognise that cyber security is not just an IT problem; it is an issue for the whole company. The following steps are typically taken when creating a cyber security strategy:

1. Identify and then quantify the risks (estimate the business impact)

2. Identify the most important information and protect it
3. Define the legal consequences of a breach
4. Create a financially based set of risk management options
5. Introduce high-level oversight to set standards of due care and review incidents
6. Implement an ongoing programme to detect, respond to and deter cyber attacks

Only the last step in this list is solely an IT issue; all the others involve other departments. The marketing and planning departments are best at estimating business impact, the legal department can define the consequences of a breach, the finance department needs to cost out the risk management options and the board should be involved in setting oversight standards. It is important to involve all parts of the company in the process of creating an enterprise-wide risk management mindset.

Part of the difficulty in establishing a cyber security strategy lies in the typically slightly adversarial relationship between the IT department and the rest of the company. Users generally expect an IT system that always works perfectly and, since all networks, in practice, must fall short of this ideal, the IT department will always be blamed and moaned about. On the other hand, the IT department typically views users as overly demanding, technologically illiterate oafs, worthy only of contempt or condescending advice such as 'have you tried turning it on yet?'. The IT department attempts to control users' behaviour through a set of policies and procedures. If these aren't followed (which they rarely are), then it's not the techies fault and the blame can be placed back squarely on the user.

What is required is a change in culture. The key to cyber security lies in the behaviour of users. In relation to changing behaviour, psychologists always advise using a carrot in preference to a stick. So, rather than enforcing a set of policies backed up by the threat of disciplinary action, a better approach is to focus on rewards, education and leading by example. Most companies want employees who are able to take the initiative and think for themselves. Self-motivated employees will optimise the task in front of them, eliminating wasted effort. So if the IT security procedures seem like a pointless obstacle to getting more business, they'll be ignored. The first step to better information security is to put the cyber threat in context. People need to understand *why* they are doing something before they'll do it.

Ultimately, information security isn't about a piece of software or an IT policy; it should be viewed as a 'way of working', a set of behaviours, a mindset. There are several different aspects to developing this new way of working. First, the whole company needs to be more aware of the risks of cyber attack and what actions can be taken to mitigate them. Second, high-risk individuals (including senior executives) need to be identified and taught a new set of behaviours. This can be carried out during lunchtime events, seminars, focus groups, workshops and so on. Third, a set of critical occasions need to be defined. These are moments during the normal working day in which the correct actions are particularly important; that is, periods of maximum vulnerability to cyber attack. Examples include leaving your desk for lunch, working from home, choosing a password or entering the office building. From a slightly longer-term perspective, project handovers, employees joining or leaving the firm, sign-offs and completions are also events that are more susceptible to cyber attack. A particular set of behaviours can be followed at these vulnerable times. These suggestions may all seem fairly obvious, but a set of small changes through which to instil good habits are the foundation stones for a wholesale change in corporate culture at a higher level.

The emphasis should be on leading by example. So often in companies, a gap exists between what is written in the corporate vision statement or policy and how people actually act in practice. The hypocrisy is particularly acute when a senior manager is flouting their own directives. Employees tend to observe the actions of their peers and follow them in preference to whatever is written in a corporate communique. As a senior manager, you do not 'communicate' a policy by writing it down and sending it to everybody by email. You communicate it by doing it; you must lead from the top.

In conclusion, information security is all about changing behaviours so, in a sense, it is as much an HR issue as an IT one. It would be farcical to ask the HR department to go round installing Microsoft Word software on employees' PCs. Is it any less farcical to expect the IT department to single-handedly change employee attitudes and behaviours? Cyber security is an issue that needs to be addressed holistically, top-down and with all departments playing their part. One way to change people's perceptions of the issue is to reconfigure the budgeting process. If the information security budget remains just a subset of the overall IT budget, it will always remain an 'IT problem'. Recategorising the need for cyber security would send a clear signal that it is a group-wide issue.

To end on a brighter note, consider this. The cyber threat is a significant new challenge looming on the corporate horizon, rooted in new technology and its attendant baffling acronyms. Cyber crime is perpetrated from the shadows by anonymous hackers; silent, often undetected but potent with malice. However, it transpires that much of this risk is the result of ignorance; lack of knowledge is itself the biggest threat. Head office is often ignorant of the extent and complexity of the corporate IT estate, users are undereducated about appropriate, safe behaviour, IT staff may not be up to date with the latest hacking techniques and exploits and the board may be struggling to get its collective head around the dimensions of the problem. The good news is that this situation is fairly easy and cheap to rectify. Improving corporate awareness can dramatically reduce cyber risk.

So we end near to where we started, having come full circle around the compass of corporate risk. The key to mitigating the cyber threat lies in mastering the 'unknown knowns', which we discussed in Chapter 1.

Conclusion

THAT COMPLETES OUR TOUR AROUND THE COMPASS POINTS OF CORPOrate risk as set out in Figure 1. We have looked at the threats that an organisation faces from all angles: public sector, private sector, internal and external. We conclude that, while all corporate crises are different in their specific details, they all share some common elements. A workable strategy for dealing with a crisis can thus be summed up in five general rules:

1. Don't deny anything before you are in full possession of the facts
2. Your response time must be faster than the speed of the story
3. When the crisis happens, bring in external consultants
4. To prevent recurrence, change the culture as well as the policies
5. You can't clear your own name; only other people can do that for you

Beware the 'unknown knowns'. These are facts that someone lower down in the organisation knows but of which senior management are unaware. Many of the case studies have involved press statements denying facts that, on further investigation, proved to be true. NASA's first instinct was to deny that the cold weather had anything to do with the *Challenger* disaster when, in fact, it was the main cause. Standard Chartered 'strongly rejected' the accusations of fraudulent misconduct in Iranian transactions made by the New York regulator but barely a month later acknowledged and accepted responsibility 'for past knowing and wilful criminal conduct in violating US economic sanctions'.

Public opinion is often sympathetic to a company in the initial stages of a corporate crisis. After all, accidents happen to everyone. But if the company denies something that later proves to be true, it's extremely damaging to the corporate brand. Reputational risk is thus not generated by the crisis per se but by the attempt to cover it up. An event that comes 'out of the blue' is clearly unforeseen, but an untruthful corporate denial can only lead to one of two conclusions in the mind of the public. Either senior management was deliberately lying or they were unaware of what was actually happening inside the company and therefore not really in control. Both of these conclusions imply that whoever is running the company should be sacked.

The 'unknown knowns' are also key to managing cyber risk. The biggest component of cyber risk is actually ignorance of that risk. The IT department is probably fully aware of the dangers posed by hackers but other departments and senior management often don't take it very seriously. Education and internal training can fix this fairly simply and cheaply.

The PR cycle is becoming increasingly faster and keeping on top of how a story develops in the media is crucial. In BP's case, relations with the press were disastrous and led to the demise of the CEO Tony Hayward. In contrast, Tesco and Boeing handled their supply chain crises in an effective manner and their brand reputations were quick to recover.

External consultants, who bring an unbiased view to the situation, are essential to crisis management. When a crisis occurs, the instinctive reaction of most managers inside the company is either how to avoid blame by pointing the finger at someone else or how to look good by telling the boss what he wants to hear. Sometimes a crisis may even be seen as an opportunity to overthrow the CEO. The more egotistical the CEO, the less likely he is to ask for external assistance and the more likely to rely on internal 'yes' men. This can be a fatal mistake, as the example of Dick Fuld and the collapse of Lehman Brothers demonstrates.

In the aftermath of a crisis, most companies introduce a raft of new policies to demonstrate that they have done something to prevent such incidents in the future. The only silver lining of a crisis, where there is one, is the chance to learn from your mistakes. However, policies on their own aren't enough. It's often easy to circumvent them or simply ignore them altogether. What's needed is a change in corporate culture. Without it, a similar crisis is likely to occur in future, as illustrated by NASA's second shuttle disaster. The *Columbia* shuttle explosion was the result of the same flawed decision-making process as had caused the *Challenger* tragedy 17 years earlier.

In summary, these are the key steps involved in dealing with a corporate crisis:

1. Acknowledge the crisis quickly and publicly, stating that you're determined to find out the facts. Make it clear that you'll take firm action but only after the truth has been established.

2. Hire external crisis management consultants and legal advisors to handle the PR and regulatory aspects of the crisis.

3. Set up a fact-finding mission composed mainly of external experts who are both well respected and well known. These are the people who will be able to clear your name, eliminate conflicts of interest and demonstrate transparency to the general public. Set out a clear timetable for this group, including deadlines for the completion of investigations and actions to be taken.

4. Keep quiet and wait for the report to come in.

5. Use the report as the basis for a widespread change in corporate culture rather than a mere change in policies so as to prevent future crises.

Notes

1. 'Man in the News: Tony Hayward', by Ed Crooks, *Financial Times*, 30 April 2010.
2. Charlie Gall, 'Piper Alpha disaster 25 years on: Survivor tells how he fled to Australia in bid to escape haunting horrors of tragedy', *Daily Record*, 8 July 2013.
3. Tim Webb, 'BP boss admits job on the line over Gulf oil spill', *Guardian*, 14 May 2010.
4. 'BP chief Tony Hayward "set to stand down"', BBC News, 26 July 2010.
5. Emmanuel Olaoye, 'JPMorgan was warned risk management not up to task', Reuters, 15 May 2012.
6. John Noble Wilford, 'Challenger, Disclosure and an 8th Casualty For NASA', *New York Times*, 14 February 1986.
7. Carol Hymowitz and Thomas Black, 'McNerney Tested at Boeing as 787 Inquiry Raises Costs', *Bloomberg*, 22 January 2013.
8. Tesco PLC, 'Tesco comments on FSAI beef survey', 15 January 2013.
9. Anna Edwards, 'Contaminated burgers made in Poland', *Daily Mail*, 30 January 2013.
10. Gordon Rayner, Robert Winnett and Christopher Hope, 'Prime Minister attacks stores over horse meat scandal', *Daily Telegraph*, 14 February 2013.
11. Andrew Clark and Elana Schor, 'Your company is bankrupt, you keep $480m. Is that fair?', *Guardian*, 7 October 2008.

12 'Standard Chartered seeks collective Iran settlement with other US regulators', *Telegraph*, 15 August 2012.
13 Helia Ebrahimi and Kamal Ahmed, 'Standard Chartered investor turns on bank for paying $340m fine', *Telegraph*, 18 August 2012.
14 Louise Armitstead, 'Standard Chartered forced to apologise for calling US sanction breaches a "clerical error"', *Telegraph*, 21 March 2013.
15 Standard Chartered PLC Press release RNS No: 5331A, 21 March 2013.
16 Ed Vulliamy, 'How a big US bank laundered millions', *Observer*, 3 April 2011.
17 Steve Boggan, 'We want British justice, not a US witchhunt', *The Times*, 3 February 2005.
18 Siri Schubert and T. Christian Miller, 'At Siemens, Bribery Was Just a Line Item', *New York Times*, 20 December 2008.
19 Susan S. Sibley, 'Rotting Apples or a Rotting Barrel', National Academy of Engineering, National Academy of Science, National Science Foundation, Workshop on Professional Ethics Education, August 2008; *MIT Faculty Newsletter*, Vol XXI, No. 5, Summer 2009.
20 'The Siemens scandal: Bavarian baksheesh', *The Economist*, 17 December 2008.
21 Richard Milne, 'Post-Its used to hide Siemens' illegal activity, says defendant', *Financial Times*, 27 May 2008.
22 Siri Schubert and T. Christian Miller, 'At Siemens, Bribery Was Just a Line Item', *New York Times*, 20 December 2008.
23 Mark Milner, 'Bribery trial: Judge criticises Siemens for failures that let fraud flourish', *The Guardian*, 29 July 2008.
24 Siri Schubert and T. Christian Miller, 'At Siemens, Bribery Was Just a Line Item', *The New York Times*, 20 December 2008.
25 Mike Esterl, David Crawford and David Reilly, 'KPMG Germany's Failure to Spot Siemens Problems Raises Questions', *The Wall Street Journal*, 24 February 2007.

26 Siri Schubert and T. Christian Miller, 'At Siemens, Bribery Was Just a Line Item', *The New York Times*, 20 December 2008.
27 Siri Schubert and T. Christian Miller, 'At Siemens, Bribery Was Just a Line Item', *The New York Times*, 20 December 2008.
28 Mike Esterl, David Crawford and Nathan Koppel, 'Siemens Internal Review Hits Hurdles: Costly Yearlong Probe By New York Law Firm Turns Up Little Clarity', *Wall Street Journal*, 23 January 2008.
29 Rachel Louise Ensign, 'Former Siemens Execs Get Record Bribery Fines', *Wall Street Journal*, 6 February 2014.
30 Carter Dougherty, 'Chief of Siemens Pledges to Streamline Operations', *New York Times*, 6 July 2007.
31 'UBS fined £29.7m by FSA over Kweku Adoboli case', BBC News, 26 November 2012.
32 Speech by Alan Greenspan to the National Italian American Foundation, Washington, D.C. 12 October 2005 (www.federalreserve.gov).
33 British Law Society, *The Whistleblowing Framework* (2013).
34 Barbara Ettorre, 'Whistleblowers: Who's the real bad guy?', Vol. 83, *Management Review*, 05-01-1994, p 18.
35 Simon Neville, 'Hero or pariah? A whistleblower's dilemma', *Guardian*, 22 November 2012.
36 'Sir James Crosby resigns from FSA', BBC News, 11 February 2009.
37 Simon Neville, 'Hero or pariah? A whistleblower's dilemma', *The Guardian*, 22 November 2012.
38 Reporters Without Borders, *World Press Freedom Index 2014*.
39 'Less guff, more puff', *The Economist*, 18 May 2013.
40 Saya Weissman, 'Bank Of America's Epic Twitter Fail', Digiday, 11 July 2013.
41 Jon Robbins, 'One Writ Too Far', *The Big Issue*, 27 February 1996.
42 Katerina Lorenzatos Makris, 'Recipe for disaster: Butterball's poor training and pay for turkey farm workers', examiner.com, 30 November 2012.

43 'Brent Spar: Battle that launched modern activism', Ethical Corporation, 5 May 2010.
44 'The parable of the Clyde', *The Economist*, 31 August 2013.
45 Marc Kaufman, 'New Allies on The Amazon', *Washington Post*, 24 April 2007.
46 Peter Dolle, 'Can Big Business Partner With NGOs?', www.knowledge.insead.edu, 25 April 2012.
47 'Air France denies spying on travelers', *New York Times*, 14 September 1991.

Index

ABC 158
Abu Ghraib 20, 112
accountants 96; 'Big Four' 72; *see also* Ernst & Young; KPMG
Adair, Red 4
Adams, Stanley 113
Adamson, Clive 106
Adoboli, Kweku 92, 101–5
Advanced Persistent Threat (APT) attacks 170–71, 180–81, 186
advertising: slots 147; Advertising Standards Authority (ASA) 62
Aesop 128
Africa 70, 81, 150, 190
'agency risk' 103
Air Commerce Act 56
Air India 53, 55
Airbus 55
Aldi 59–61
al-Gaddafi, Colonel Mu'ammar 151
All Nippon Airways (ANA) 51–52, 55
Amazon 176
America *see* USA
American Civil Liberties Union 189
American Civil War 15
Amnesty International 149, 151
Andersen, Arthur E. 8–10, 13
animal welfare 157–61
anti-discrimination legislation 125

Anti-Money Laundering (AML) 138
Anti-Monopoly Bureau 81
AOL/Time Warner 132
Apollo programme 41
appellation contrôlée 57
Apple 81, 173, 184
Apps 81
Arbroath smokies 57
Ardennes 16
Argentina 93, 134
Ariane space rockets 40
Arthur Andersen 8–9
Asia 71, 73, 156, 166; markets crisis 131
Asia Pacific region 142
Athens, Olympic Games 93
Audi 147
Australia 70, 142, 153
Austria 153
Autonomy 121
Axis of Evil 79, 169

Baker-Bates, Rodney 106
Ballinger, Jeff 154
Baltimore Ravens 146
Bam 166
Bangladesh 93
Bank for International Settlement (BIS) 82

Bank Melli 72, 74
Bank of America 148
Bank of England 71
Bank of West Africa 71
Bank Saderat 72, 74
bankruptcy/bankruptcies 65, 133; Barings 123; Lehman Brothers 65–68; Enron 8
banks 31, 72, 79, 83, 121, 129, 138; Bank Secrecy Act 72; Barings 123; BCCI 79; Central Bank of Iran/Markazi 72, 74; Citibank 77; Co-operative 106–7; Eastern 70; Export-Import 98; Federal reserve 72, 77; for International Settlement (BIS) 82; HBOS 118–19; HSBC 73–74; ING 73; interbank loans 82; Ionian 70; JPMorgan 12, 13, 130; Lehman Brothers 40–41, 65–68, 120, 126, 197; Lloyds TSB 92; NatWest 87; Melli 72, 74; of America 148; of England 71; of West Africa 71; Parliamentary Commission on Banking Standards 118; Saderat 72, 74; Saudi Arabian 73; Standard Chartered 69, 70–80, 83, 195; UBS 92, 101–5; World 98, 100; *see also* NatWest Three
Barings 123
BBC 119
BCCI 79
Begg, Moazzam 152
Beijing 26; Anti-Monopoly Bureau 81
Belgium 16, 153; *see also* Congo: Belgian
benefits 135
Berkeley (University of California) 162
Berkshire Hathaway 80
Bermingham, David 86–87

BETonSPORTS 85
Birkenfeld, Bradley 121
Blair, Tony 105
blogs 26, 111
Bock, Ulrich 99
Boehner, John 139
Boeing 49, 68, 196; Dreamliner 40, 49–56
Bohr, Niels 21
Bombay 70
bonds 131
bonuses 78
Booz Allen Hamilton 172
Boston 52, 53
Botnets 175–76
Botswana 190
BP 1–5, 13, 196; *see also Deepwater Horizon* disaster; Hayward, Tony
Bradford council 106
Brazil 190; rainforest 164
Brégier, Fabrice 55
Brent Spar 160–61
bribery 91, 93–98, 126; Anti-Bribery Convention 99; Bribery Act 89, 98; *see also* corruption
Brigham City 42
'bring your own technology' (BYOT) 184, 187
Britain 28, 72, 85, 87, 134, 151, 160, 163, 176; empire 27, 70
British American Tobacco 167
Browne, Lord 1; *see also* BP
Brunei 142
Buffett, Warren 80, 91
Burberry 71
bureaucracy 26–29, 30, 31, 34, 35; *see also* red tape
Burger King 109, 159
Burgundy 57
Burke, Edmund 133

Burma 75, 127
Bush, George W. 4, 169
Butterball 157–58

Cadbury, William 151
Calcutta 70
California 68; University of (Berkeley) 162
Cambridge 159
Cameron International Corp 3
Cameron, David 61
Cameroon 71
Canada 88, 142, 153, 158
Cape Canaveral 43
Cape Province 70
Cargill 165
Carroll, David 109
Carruthers, David 85, 87–89
Cathy, Dan 110
caveat emptor principle 143, 145
Cayman Islands 87
Central Bank of Iran/Markazi 72, 74
Challenger space shuttle disaster 39–49, 195, 197; causes of 41–49
Champagne region 57
Channel 4 153, 154
Chardonnay 57
Chartered Financial Analyst (CFA) Institute 130
Charybdis, riddle of 143–45
Chicago 110, 157
Chick-fil-A 110
Chile 142
China 1, 27, 28, 70, 80–81, 84, 93, 119, 124, 171–74, 142, 189; opium trade 69; People's Liberation Army (PLA) 170, 171, 174, 178
Cisco Systems 175
Citibank 77
Clarke, Philip 60, 62–63

Clinton, Bill 71
Clyde: Firth of 163; River 163–64
CNBC 54
CNN 4, 26, 109
Coca-Cola 173
collateralised debt obligation (CDO) 64–67, 144
Colombia 1
Columbia space shuttle disaster 48, 197
COMESA 81
Comic Relief UK 152
Comigel 60, 61
compliance assessment areas 106
Computer Misuse Act (1990) 188
Condé Nast 67
Congo: Belgian 150, 150–51; Reform Association 151, 161
Conlumino 63
Conrad, Joseph 151
consultants 9, 29–36, 38
Co-operative Bank 106–7
corporate: crisis 68; social responsibility (CSR) 156
corruption 98, 100, 101, 106, 126, 133; *see also* bribery
Costa Rica 85
Costco Wholesale 159
Cragg, James 131
crashes, financial 130; 2008 71, 130, 131, 34; Asia (1997) 31; Black Monday (1987) 131; Flash (2010) 131; Great (1929) 65
Crigger, Gary 114
crises 17, 25, 29–36, 38, 40, 95–97, 99–101, 123, 131, 160, 161, 195, 197; Eurozone 104
crisis management 24, 25, 37–38; five key principles of 15–38
Crosby, Sir James 118, 120

culture, corporate 36–38;
    can corporate culture ever
    change? 32–34
CultureMetrics 107
Cutty Sark whisky 57
Cyber Intelligence Sharing and
    Protection Act (CISPA) 189
cyber threat 13, 17, 169–93
Cyprus 70

Daily Express 60
Daily Mail 59
Daily Mirror 60
Daily Telegraph 59, 76, 77, 150
Dalepak Hambleton 59
Dallas airport 85
Darby, Giles 86
Darby, Sergeant Joseph M. 112
Darwin, Charles 32
data citadels 183, 186–87
Data Protection Act (1998) 188
Dawson, Jo 119
Debevoise & Plimpton 99
Deepwater Horizon disaster 1–3
Delaware, University of, John L.
    Weinberg Center for Corporate
    Governance 55
Deloitte 72–73
Denny's 159
Department of Agriculture, Food and
    the Marine (Ireland) 58
Department of Education (USA) 157
Department of Financial Services
    (DFS) (New York State)
    69, 72–76
Department of Health (UK) 58
Department of Health and Human
    Services (USA) 157
Department of Justice (USA)
    87, 97–98

deregulation of financial services,
    1986 130
Deutsche Post/DHL 166
Devine, Thomas 116
Dimon, Jamie 12
disasters: *Challenger* space shuttle
    39–49, 195, 197; *Columbia* space
    shuttle 48, 197; *Deepwater Horizon*
    1–3; Hurricane Katrina 4; *Piper
    Alpha* 3
distributed denial of service (DDoS)
    attacks 176
Dodd-Frank Act 11, 126, 131
Doha 142
Dolata, Uwe 96
Domino's 108–12
Dorgan, Senator Bryon 8
dot.com bubble 131, 132
Downey, Tom 53
downstream customers 33
Doyle, Sir Arthur Conan 151
Dreamliner 40, 49–56
Dudley, Bob 5
Duncan, David 10
Dunnes Stores 59

East India Company 131
Eastern Bank 70
eBay 184
Eckard, Cheryl 121
Economist, The 146, 163
Edinburgh International Television
    Festival 161
EEC *see* European Union
'effects doctrine' 89
eggs 159; egg cup and the pea 20–26,
    29; salmonella in 58
Egypt 84
Elder Dempster 150
Electronic Frontier Foundation 189

Elson, Charles 54
emails 81, 184–85, 193; *see also* spam
employees, rogue 12, 91–122, 155, 166; *see also* whistleblowers
Energy Companies Obligation 137
England 83
Enlightenment 28, 127
Enron 6–8, 10, 13, 87, 126, 131
Environment and Development Economics 162
equal opportunities 30–31
Ernst & Young 66, 156
ethics 105–8
Ethiopia 81; Ethiopian Air 53
eugenics 32
European Court of Justice 89
European Union 86, 89, 113, 139, 141, 142, 189; *see also* crises: Eurozone; Single European Market
exchange-traded funds (ETFs) 103–4
Experian 71
Export–Import Bank 98
extraterritorial: reach 83–85; legislation 69–90

Facebook 26, 81, 147, 177
Fair Labor Association 156
Falklands War 134
False Claims Act 121
Farrakhan, Louis 151
Fastow, Andrew 7, 87
FBI 98, 121, 159
Federal Aviation Administration (FAA) 52–56
Federal Reserve 72, 77
FedEx 109
feedback control loop 22–23, 25, 33
Ferrari 179
Feynman, Richard 44–45

Financial Conduct Authority (FCA) 12, 106, 136
Financial Services Act (2012) 133–34
Financial Services Authority (FSA) 71, 76, 87, 102, 120, 138
Findus 60–61
Finland 89
Firestone 114–18
First World War 15–16, 50
fishing industry 163
Fletcher, James 41–42
Florida 39, 42, 114
Flowers, Paul 106
Food Safety Authority of Ireland (FSAI) 58
Forbes Magazine 148
Ford 114–18
Foreign Corrupt Practices Act (FCPA) 87–88, 94, 98, 99
Forest Stewardship Council (FSC) 165
Fortune 6
France 16, 51, 89–90, 124, 141, 153, 178
Frank, Barney 85
fraud 103; Serious Fraud Office (SFO) 87
Friedrich, Matthew W. 98
Friends of the Earth 162
Friesland, the Netherlands 140
FTSE 62, 76
Fuld, Dick 65, 67–68, 197
Fulton, Maureen 1
Furnham, Adrian 107
futures trading 134

gagging clauses 119–20
Gambia 71
GCSE grades 35
Genel Energy 5

General Agreement on Tariffs and
    Trade (GATT) 141–42
General Electric (GE) 53
General Motors 178
Germany 16, 94, 100, 151, 153, 160;
    Deutsche Post/DHL 166; German
    Exchange Act 1896 134
Ghana 71
Glasgow 163, 186
GlaxoSmithKline 121
Glencore 81
Glenfiddich whisky 57
Global Settlement 131
globalisation 83; the end of 80–86
GM technology 162
golden rice 161–63
Google 108, 171; Google Earth 177
Gore, Al 151
Government Accountability Project
    (GAP) 116
Great Crash (1929) 65
Great Depression 16
Great Train Robbery 186
Great Universal Stores (GUS) 71
Greece 93, 94, 104, 124
Greenpeace 138, 160–65, 167
Greenspan, Alan 103
Greenwich, University of 113
Grierson, Christopher 92
Groupe Bull 178
Guantánamo Bay 84, 151
Guardian, The 59, 172
Gulf of Mexico 70

hackers/hacking 86, 178, 180, 187–
    90, 196; *see also* McKinnon, Gary
hacktivists 174–76, 182
Haffey, Barbara 114
Haiti, earthquake in 166
Halliburton 2–3

Hamilton, Benedict 121
Hammer, Arnold 3–4
Hammonds, Kirsty 108
Hardy, Jeremy 154
Harper, Jessica 92
Harper's Magazine 154
Hawaii 172
Hayward, Tony 1–5, 196; *see also* BP;
    Deepwater Horizon disaster
HBOS 118–19
health and safety regulations 125
healthcare standards 37
Heinz 80–81
Hershman, Michael 99
Hewlett-Packard 121
Hilton 178
Hitchcock, Alfred 172
Hizb ut-Tahrir 151
HMV 109
Hoffman-La Roche 113
Hogan Lovells 92
Hogan personality profiling
    system 107
Hogan, Alan 114–17
Homer 127
Hong Kong 11, 69–70, 83
Hong Kong Telecom 132
Hornby, Andy 118
House of Commons 132
House of Lords 132
Houston Natural Gas 5
HR 106, 107, 111, 117, 126, 170, 193
HSBC 73–74
HTML 8182
Huerta, Michael 52
Hughes Commission 134
Humane Society 159
Huntingdon Life Sciences (HLS) 159
Hurricane Katrina 4
Hybrid Turkeys 157–58

IBM 178
Iceland 59
Immigration Bill (USA) 139
Independent, The 59
India 51, 70, 131, 142, 149, 162, 175; Air India 53, 54
Indian Ocean, tsunamis in 165–66
Indonesia 156
industrial espionage 113, 179
Information Commissioner's Office 188
ING 73
insider trading 130
intellectual property (IP) 173
International Monetary Fund 82
InterNorth 5
Ionian Bank 70
Iran 69, 71–75, 79, 83, 166, 195; Iranian Transactions Regulations 71
Iraq 5, 84; invasion of 19; weapons of mass destruction (WMD) 17, 19, 170; *see also* Abu Ghraib
Ireland 58–60, 153; Food Safety Authority of (FSAI) 58
Israel 93, 153
IT 9, 170, 180–84, 190–93, 196
Italy 51, 93, 124, 127, 153

Jackson, Cynthia 114
Jackson, General 'Stonewall' 15
Japan 51, 142, 153; All Nippon Airways (ANA) 51–52, 55; equity bubble 131; Japan Airlines 52, 55; Japanese Transport Ministry 53
Johannesburg 70
John L. Weinberg Center for Corporate Governance (University of Delaware) 55
Johnnie Walker whisky 57
Johnson, Boris 76

Jordan, Michael 155
JPMorgan 12, 13, 130

Kazakhstan 84–85, 88
Keith, Mr Justice 103
Kennedy, John Fitzgerald 42
Kimberley, South Africa 70
Kipling, Rudyard 173
Kleinfeld, Klaus 99
Knight, Phil 155
Know Your Client (KYC) regulations 138
known: knowns 154; unknowns 17–19
KPMG 96–97
Kroll 121
Kutschenreuter, Michael 96

Lake Geneva 146
LAN Airlines 53
Langert, Bob 165
Laphroaig whisky 57
law 83–85; European 141; legal jurisdiction in cyberspace 188–90
Lawsky, Benjamin 76
Lay, Kenneth 8
Leeson, Nick 92, 102, 123
Legend Securities 68
Lehman Brothers 40–41, 65–68, 120, 126, 197
Leopold II, King 150–51
Libertini, David 158
Libya 75, 151
Lidl 59
Liffey Meats 59
LinkedIn 177
Liverpool 150
Lloyds TSB 92
loans 82
lobbying 42, 24–25
Lockwood, Timothy 114

London 75, 76, 87, 103, 128, 152, 186; City 121; Exhibition Road 140; Olympic Games 128; Stock Exchange 75
'London Whale' 12
Los Angeles 110
Löscher, Peter 99–100
LOT Polish Airlines 53
LoveFilm 81

MacGuffins 172–73
Macondo prospect 2
mad cow disease 58
Maginot Line 16
Malabar Coast 131
Malaysia 142
malware 170–71
mandarin system 26–28
Mandiant 170–71, 174, 178
Manning, Bradley 107
Marshall Islands 2
Martinez, Eduardo 166
Massachusetts Institute of Technology 93
May, Theresa 86
Mazur, Robert 79
MBA courses 21, 40
MBUSA 147
McAuliffe, Christa 39, 43; see also *Challenger* space shuttle disaster; Reagan, Ronald: 'Teacher in Space Project'
McDermott, Tracey 102
McDonald's 152–54, 159, 164–65, 167
McIntyre, Tim 108–9
McKinnon, Gary 86, 87
McKinsey 53
McLaren 170
McNerney, James 53–55
Meddings, Richard 71, 78

Medellin 79
Meier, Susanne 166
Mekjarvik, Norway 161
Melton Mowbray pork pies 57
Menendez, Jose Juan and Clotilde 114
Mercy for Animals (MFA) 157–59
Merkel, Angela 172
Merton, Robert 29
Messina, Strait of 127
Mexico 73, 93, 142; Gulf of 1, 2, 4
Microsoft 184, 193
Middle East 72, 117, 166
Milken 131
Missouri 85
Moltke, General Helmuth von 15
Monderman, Hans 140, 143
money laundering 73, 89; Anti-Money Laundering (AML) regulations 72–73, 138; Know Your Client (KYC) regulations 138
Mongolia 1
Moore, Patrick 163
Moore, Paul 119–20
Morel, Edmund Dene 150–51, 161
Morris, David 152–54
Morrison's 63
Morton-Thiokol see Thiokol
mortgages 64–65, 71, 129
Moscow 172
Mulgrew, Gary 86
Munich 91, 97; Technical University of 162
Muse 128–29
Myanmar (formerly Burma) 75

Nader, Ralph 112
name-clearing 37–38, 195
NASA 40–49, 68, 195, 197; Office of Safety, Reliability, and Quality Assurance 47; see also Apollo

programme; *Challenger* space shuttle disaster; *Columbia* space shuttle disaster
Nation of Islam 151
National Academy of Sciences 161
National Highway Traffic Safety Administration (NHTSA) 117
National Press Club 155
National Security Act (1947) 189
National Security Agency (NSA) 172, 189
NatWest 87; Three 86–90
Nestlé 146
Netherlands 140, 153, 160, 188
Neubürger, Heinz-Joachim 97
New York 11, 69, 70, 72–75, 77, 78, 83, 87–88, 99, 110, 195; New York Act 134; State 69, 72, 79; stock exchange 84, 94, 108; Wall Street 6, 121; World Trade Center 39
New York Times, The 43
New Zealand 142, 153
News Corp 118
News of the World 118
newspapers and periodicals: *Daily Express* 60; *Daily Mail* 59; *Daily Mirror* 60; *Daily Telegraph* 59, 76, 77, 150; *Economist, The* 146, 163; *Environment and Development Economics* 162; *Forbes Magazine* 148; *Fortune* 6; *Guardian* 59, 172; *Harper's Magazine* 154; *New York Times* 43; *News of the World* 118; *Science* 161; *Sun, The* 59; *The Times* 59, 87, 151; *Wall Street Journal* 11, 99, 153
NHS 35, 105, 116; NHS, 'postcode lottery' 36
Nigeria 71, 88–89, 93, 190
Nike 154–57, 164

Noll, Peter 96
non-governmental organisations (NGOs) 13, 148, 149–67
North Carolina 114
North Korea 71
North Sea 3
Northcote, Stafford 27–28
Norway 89, 161

O'Reilly, Miriam 120
Obama, Barack 4, 83, 139, 169
Obama, Michelle 157
Occidental 3
OECD 99
Office of Foreign Assets Control (OFAC) 71, 77
Ofgem 136, 137; Energy Companies Obligation 137
Ofwat 136
Olympic Games: Athens 93; London 128
Oreo 147
Organisation for Economic Co-operation and Development (OECD) 94
ORR 136

Pacific Aero Products Co. 49
Pacific Rim 142
Panic (1907) 134
Parliamentary Commission on Banking Standards 118
Parma ham 57
Paterson, John 70
Peace, Sir John 71, 78
People's Liberation Army (PLA) 170, 171, 174, 178
Persichini Jr, Joseph 98
Peru 81, 83, 142
Pierer, Heinrich von 95–96, 99

Pieth, Mark 93
Piner, Matt 63
Pinot Noir 57
Piper Alpha disaster 3
policy, gap between policy and practice 30–32
political correctness 125
Ponemon Institute 179
Port Elizabeth 70
Portugal 124
PowerPoint presentations 177
price fixing 113
Product Control Group 66–67
profit and loss account (P&L) 6–7
Project Gazelle 74
Pro-Utah 42
psychometric tests 106–7
Public Concern at Work 113
public opinion 38, 135–39

Qatar Airways 53
Qing Dynasty 27

Radial ATX tyre 115; *see also* Firestone
rainforests 164–65, 183
Reagan, Ronald 40, 42, 44, 149; 'Teacher in Space Project' 42–43
Red Cross 149, 166
Red Guards 27
red tape 139–42; *see also* bureaucracy
Renault 179
Repo 105 65–66
Reuters 129
Rice, Matt 158
Rockefeller Foundation 162
Rockwell International 49
Rogers Commission 44, 46, 49
Roquefort cheese 57
Rose Electronics 54

Rothermund, Heinz 161
Rumsfeld, Donald 17, 19–20, 112
Runkle, Nathan 158
Russia 86, 93, 119, 149, 153, 175; financial crisis (1998) 131

Saddam Hussein 19
Sainsbury's 63
San Francisco 49ers 146
Sands, Peter 71, 76, 78
Sarbanes–Oxley Act 10–11, 113, 126, 131
Saudi Arabia 73, 115
Sauven, John 165
Savings and Loan crisis (1989) 131
Schrödinger's Cat 34
Science 161
Scotland 160, 163
Scylla and Charybdis 127–28, 133, 134, 136, 148, 167; *see also* Charybdis, riddle of
Seattle 49
Second World War 16, 33
Securities and Exchange Commission (SEC) 12, 87, 88, 93, 96–99, 101, 121, 136
Serious Fraud Office 87
Setzer, Michael 108
Seward, William 104
Shanghai 70
Shaobo, Qin 187
Shell 160–61
Shetland 160
shortselling 133, 134
Sicily 127
Siekaczek, Reinhard 91–95, 97
Siemens 88, 90–101, 106, 117; Telecom-Gear unit 98
Sierra Leone 71
Silbey, Susan 93

Silvercrest Foods 59, 60
Singapore 70, 77, 124, 127, 142
Singer, Stephan 99
Single European Market 141
Sir John Barnard's Act 1734 133
Skype 81
slush funds 91, 94
Smith, Adam 103
Smith, Tim 59–61
Snowden, Edward 172, 189
Somalia 11
Sony, PlayStation 188
South Africa 70, 153, 190; British 70
South Korea 2, 51
South Sea Bubble 131–34
Southern Poverty Law Center 159
Soviet economy 107
Spain 124, 134, 153; colonies in Latin America 131
spam 175
Stalder-Olsen, Brigitte 166
Standard Chartered Bank 69–80, 83, 195
Starwood Hotels 178
Steel, Helen 152–54
Stevenson, Lord 118
stock jobbing 134
Stop Huntingdon Animal Cruelty (SHAC) 159
Sudan 75, 100
Suez Canal 70
Sui Dynasty 27
Sullom Voe 160
Sun, The 59
Super Bowl 146–47
supermarkets 57–58, 65, 144; *see also* Aldi; Iceland; Lidl; Morrison's; Sainsbury's; Tesco; Waitrose
supply chain 63; management 38, 39–68

Sweden 51
SWIFT payments 87
Switzerland 113, 153
Syngenta 162

Takamatsu Airport 52
Taliban 151
Talisker whisky 57
Target 159
target-setting 34, 111
tax 82, 93, 121, 135, 138; avoidance 135–36; 'mansion' 82
Taylor, John 107
Tehran, hostage crisis 71
Temasek 77
'terroir', concept of 56–57
terrorism 73, 75, 159, 173; 9/11 attacks 39, 86; War on Terror 169
Tesco 59, 68, 196; Everyday Value range 59, 61; horsemeat scandal 40, 58–63
Texas 4, 5, 48, 87, 114
Thailand 153
Thatcher, Margaret 4, 136
Thiokol 42, 45, 47, 48
Thomsen, Linda C. 98
Thomson Reuters 129
'threat actors' 172–79
3M 53
Tide 147
Times, The 59, 87, 151
Torquay 142
trade 102, 141, 142; futures trading 134; General Agreement on Tariffs and Trade (GATT) 141–42; slaves 131; Transatlantic Free Trade Agreement (TAFTA) 142; treaties 141; World Trade Organization (WTO) 142; Transatlantic Free Trade Agreement (TAFTA) 142

Transocean 2–3
Trans-Pacific Partnership (TPP) 142
Transparency International 99
Treasury Select Committee 119–20
Trevelyan, Charles 27–28
Trinidad 153
Trojan viruses 179
tsunamis 165–66
Tufte, Edward 45–46
Twain, Mark 151
Twitter 26, 61, 81, 108, 110, 145–48, 167, 177

UBS 92, 101–5
UK 3, 12, 31, 51, 57–61, 80, 84–89, 137, 176, 188; Advertising Standards Authority (ASA) 62; Bribery Act 89, 98; Comic Relief 152; Computer Misuse Act (1990) 188; Data Protection Act 188; Department of Health 58; Energy Companies Obligation 137; Financial Conduct Authority (FCA) 12, 106, 136; Financial Services Act 133–34; Financial Services Authority (FSA) 71, 76, 87, 102, 120, 138; Food Safety Authority 58; House of Commons 132; House of Lords 132; Huntingdon Life Sciences (HLS) 159; Information Commissioner's Office 188; Parliamentary Commission on Banking Standards 118; Public Concern at Work 113; Serious Fraud Office (SFO) 87; Sir John Barnard's Act 1734 133; Stop Huntingdon Animal Cruelty (SHAC) 159; Treasury Select Committee 119–20
United Airlines 52, 109

United Nations 149, 166; Environment Programme (UNEP) 164
United Parcel Service (UPS) 166
unknown knowns 17–20, 38, 80, 193, 195, 196; *see also* known: knowns; known: unknowns
upstream suppliers 33
Uruguay 142
USA 3, 11, 17, 41, 54, 67, 71, 73, 75–80, 84–87, 93, 96–98, 108, 110, 115, 116, 121, 124–27, 139, 142, 149, 153, 155, 157, 159, 172, 173, 176, 179, 189, 196; aerospace industry 40; Air Commerce Act 56; American Civil Liberties Union 189; Congress 4, 11, 124, 139, 148; 169; Congressional Committee 67–68; Cyber Intelligence Sharing and Protection Act (CISPA) 189; Department of Defense 47; Department of Education 157; Department of Health and Human Services 157; Department of Justice 73, 87, 97–98, 176; Dodd–Frank Act 11, 126 131; Electronic Frontier Foundation 189; Fair Labor Association 156; False Claims Act 121; FBI 98, 121, 159; Federal Aviation Administration (FAA) 52–56; Foreign Corrupt Practices Act (FCPA) 87–88, 94, 98, 99; Forest Stewardship Council (FSC) 165; Global Settlement 131; Government Accountability Project (GAP) 116; House of Representatives 139; Hughes Commission 134; Immigration Bill 139; Latin America 1, 131, 166; Midwest 183; National Academy of Sciences 161; National Highway

Traffic Safety Administration (NHTSA) 117; National Press Club 155; National Security Act (1947) 189; National Security Agency (NSA) 172, 189; New York Act 134; New York State Department of Financial Services (DFS) 69, 72, 73, 74, 75, 76; North America 142; Office of Foreign Assets Control (OFAC) 71, 77; Rockefeller Foundation 162; Sarbanes-Oxley Act 10–11, 113, 126, 131; Savings and Loan crisis (1989) 131; Securities and Exchange Commission (SEC) 12, 87, 88, 93, 97–99, 96, 101, 121; Senate 10, 73; Senate Committee Hearing 8; Senate Permanent Subcommittee on Investigations 73; Southern Poverty Law Center 159; Spanish colonies in Latin America 131; State of the Union Address 169; Super Bowl 146–47; Treasury Department 71; United Airlines 52, 109; United Parcel Service (UPS) 166; US Army Criminal Investigation Command 112; Wall Street Reform and Consumer Protection Unit 98–99
Utah 42
U-turn transactions 71–72

Van Etten, Daniel 114, 117
Venezuela 1, 93, 117
Vickers, Andrew 161
Vietnam 1, 93, 142, 155, 156, 175
Virginia 170; West Virginia University 114
vitamins 162
Volkswagen 178

Waitrose 59
Wall Street Journal, The 11, 99, 153
Wall Street Reform and Consumer Protection Unit 98–99
'War of Jenkins' Ear' 134
War on Terror 169
Washington: D.C. 98, 116, 124; State 49, 51
Wass, Sasha 103
waterholes 187
Waugh, Auberon 153
Waxman, Henry 68
Wendy's 159
Westervelt, Conrad 49
whistleblowers 112–13, 116, 119–22, 154, 155, 166
White Horse whisky 57
Wojcinski, Helen 158
Wordsworth, William 145
'work to rule' concept 31
World Bank 98, 100
World Economic Forum 124, 127
World Trade Organization (WTO) 142
World Wide Fund for Nature (WWF) 149, 165
World Wide Web 81

Xstrata 81

Y2K bug 173
Yahoo 89–90
YouGov 135
YouTube 108
Yuasa 54

Zambia 190
Zimbabwe 77, 81, 127